The Prediction Book of Practical Magic

The Prediction Book of

PRACTICAL MAGIC

Michael Howard

JAVELIN BOOKS
LONDON · NEW YORK · SYDNEY

First published in the U.K. 1986 by Javelin Books,
Artillery House, Artillery Row, London SW1P 1RT

Reprinted 1988

Distributed in the United States by
Sterling Publishing Co., Inc.,
2 Park Avenue, New York, N.Y. 10016.

Distributed in Australia by
Capricorn Link (Australia) Pty Ltd.,
PO Box 665, Lane Cove, NSW 2066

British Library Cataloguing in Publication Data

Howard, Michael, *1948-*
   Practical magic.
   1. Occult sciences
   I. Title
   133   BF1411

   ISBN 0-7137-1682-7

ISBN 0 7137 1682 7

Typeset by Poole Typesetting (Wessex) Ltd.
Printed and bound in Great Britain by
The Guernsey Press Co., Guernsey, C.I.

Contents

Introduction

The purpose of this book is to present a basic primer of magic designed for modern people. The way magic works and the results which an ordinary person can obtain through the use of magical techniques will be explained in simple everyday terms.

The practice of magic is as old as humanity. In the Stone Age the first hunters made models of the animals they hoped to catch the next day. These models were pierced with arrows in a symbolic act to ensure that the hunt was a success. The construction of the model and the rituals practised by the prehistoric magicians created a sympathetic link between the hunters and their prey. These cave hunters performed this ritual not because they were ignorant or primitive people but because they believed that by such symbolic magical acts they could influence their environment. This belief has been a central tenet of magical philosophy through the ages.

For far too long magic has been regarded as little more than an ancient superstition. The reason for this is not difficult to understand. The practice of magic was for many centuries regarded as evil. It was specifically forbidden by strict religious and criminal laws which restricted what people could believe in. In such a repressive atmosphere anyone who claimed to be a magician or an occultist (a person who studies hidden knowledge) could face at best severe censure and at worst the actual loss of his/her life. This led to magic becoming an underground occupation. It was performed clandestinely by private individuals and secret societies who jealously guarded the knowledge they possessed from the outside world.

Magic has such a sinister image today because it was practised in secret for so many hundreds of years. It is natural that if people do not have access to any real knowledge of a subject they invent sensational stories to explain its secrecy. With the revival of interest in all aspects of the occult over the last 20 years, combined with a more liberated religious atmosphere, the practice of magic has gradually left the shadows and come out into the open. With our increased knowledge of the past it is now possible to produce forms of practical magic which are relevant to our modern age yet still preserve the traditional values of ancient magical philosophy.

To the average person the word magic will either conjure up a vision of a circus conjuror producing a rabbit from a top hat or a hooded figure chanting demonic spells in a country graveyard. Both these images are false ones. The root from which the word magic is derived means quite simply 'wisdom'. The first historical use of the word referred to the Magi, an ancient sect of Persian priests who were adepts in the occult arts of astrology, divination and magical practice. The three Magi, or wise men, who brought symbolic gifts to the new-born Jesus belonged to this ancient priesthood of magicians.

Over the centuries magic has developed in various ways in accordance with cultural changes and the different attitudes of the people who have practised the art. These different forms of magic will be reflected in the contents of this book. It should be made clear that you do not have to belong to any particular religious faith to be a practising magician. Obviously magic has become associated with many religious beliefs during its history. All the major religions contain elements of magical practice. The Catholic Mass is one well-known example. Although you do not have to be a religious person, in the accepted sense of the term, it would be almost impossible for any true magician to be completely successful without having some personal belief in a Supreme Being or the existence of a spiritual reality beyond the limits of the physical senses.

Magic can be practised not only as a means of creating stable or improved conditions in the environment around the magician but it is a well-tested method for personal growth and spiritual development. It should never be treated as a pastime to make life more exciting, just another hobby like stamp collecting, or as an easy route to material comfort. Those who decide to follow the magical path should adopt the highest moral principles. The practice of magic is a very serious undertaking which carries a large degree of responsibility. Above all, practising any form of magic, even at its

8

most simple level, will reveal all kinds of things about yourself. On the door of every magician's temple or working place should be engraved in letters of fire the immortal words written above the gateway of the Delphic oracle in ancient Greece 'Man, Know Thyself'.

The seeker who approaches the practice of magic with a positive attitude and with a dedication to work hard for the end results will find a new world of exciting and satisfying experiences will open up before him. Follow us as we take the first steps on the magical path to self-enlightenment.

1 Magical Principles

Magic is only a mysterious subject if you know nothing about it. Therefore any form of practical instruction about magic must begin by defining exactly what it is. One famous definition of magic says that it is the science and art of using little-known natural forces to achieve changes in consciousness and the physical environment in accordance with the will of the individual. Although slightly long-winded this statement can be taken as a starting point in our quest to define what magic really is all about.

To a person who left school without any educational qualifications the study of physics, for instance, will be a closed subject to him or her. However, providing he is fairly intelligent he could grasp the fundamentals of even that most difficult field of study. Magic is the same because the beginner is faced with volumes of seemingly incomprehensible literature. Most of this literature is written in obscure technical terms which act as a barrier to the outsider. In order to unravel the mysteries of this magical labyrinth we shall start with the basics of the subject.

The universe

The magician looks at the universe in a way which is radically different from the average non-magical person. To the practitioner of magic the universe is not a clockwork model driven by purely physical forces as is imagined by the materialist. The magical universe is far more mysterious and awesome because it is inhabited by forces and energies which are invisible to our present scientific technology but are no less real than any product of the physicist's laboratory.

The person who practises magic does not regard the physical world as the only reality but as the visible manifestation of a greater spiritual reality. Neither is the universe a chaotic battleground of uncontrollable forces but it has a cosmic pattern which can be understood by those who possess the symbolic key to its secrets. This key is to be found in the theory of magical correspondences and is enshrined in the well-known Hermetic maxim, 'As above, so below'.

According to ancient legend the following words were carved on an emerald tablet which was discovered in a cave that was believed to be the last resting place of the Greek deity Hermes Trismegitus, or Thrice Greatest, who was the patron god of magicians: 'That which is above is like that which is below and that which is below is like that which is above to achieve the wonders of the one thing.'

This saying indicates that the physical world is a reflection of the spiritual realm. God represents the macrocosm or greater universe while man is the microcosm or smaller universe. The 'one thing' in the Hermetic maxim is the life force which sustains and permeates the universe. This ancient truth can only be understood properly by realising that the spiritual and the material are aspects of the same reality.

Everything in the universe contains the life force to a greater or lesser extent. Under normal circumstances we are not even aware of the workings of this creative principle, except perhaps in its most basic form as the urge to reproduce our species or in the daily struggle for survival in the physical world. The magician is aware of the life force as an energy field existing both within and outside himself. Combined with the use of the subconscious mind, which is the messenger between the material and spiritual realms, the trained magician can use this force to produce what outsiders might regard as magical effects. In fact the magician is working with quite natural forces and there is nothing supernatural or paranormal about the results he achieves as you will realise as we progress along the magical path.

Good and evil

It should be stressed that magic is not 'good' or 'evil' in itself. The energy used by the magician is neutral. It has been compared to electricity which is freely available to boil a kettle but if misused can cause serious injury or damage. It is the use to which it is put that make it either beneficial or destructive — the power is the same. Because magical energy is not good or evil in itself the apprentice magician must be spiritually mature enough to use it only for positive ends.

Obviously the temptation to misuse occult knowledge is strong in some less developed people although magic does have a fail-safe mechanism built into it to prevent this type of misuse. It is an old axiom that anyone who uses magical techniques for negative purposes will discover that the power raised will return to the sender threefold. This is a powerful incentive only to work positively. The proper application of magical expertise involves maintaining the correct ethical attitude which allows positive spiritual energy to flow through you.

Essential points for the student

A prerequisite for working any form of magic is a positive frame of mind. You must cultivate a mental state in which you believe that anything, within reasonable limits, is possible. The only limitations on what you can achieve are those formed in your imagination which creates images of failure. Novices who try out magical techniques for the first time sometimes do not get the results they seek. Naturally, as a bad workman blames his tools, they think it is because the materials they used were unsuitable or the instructions they were given were not correct.

Although this may be the answer in some cases the cause for such failure frequently lies closer to home and in reality stems from the practitioner's own lack of faith and confidence in the ability to make things happen — to create magic in fact. To really make magic work you must believe in yourself and in what you are doing. People who are sceptical about the efficaciousness of magic or even the existence of unseen influences which have an effect on their life will never make successful magicians.

In the old days the student was encouraged to develop what is termed the magical personality. This is an idealized version of yourself as you would like others to see you. The technique sometimes involved selecting a magical name indicating that your personality had changed. This is sound psychology because the aspiring magician who identifies with Merlin or Morgan Le Fay may well believe that he/she is capable of achieving similar levels of magical expertise as these legendary characters.

Students of the magical art must learn to open themselves up to the force flowing through the universe. It has been said that magic is the art of weaving unseen forces into form. The magician tunes into the force and 'borrows' a certain amount of the surplus which is available from this great cosmic reservoir of raw natural energy.

This energy is concentrated, focused and channelled using magical images which at first only exist in the imagination or astral realm. When the magician directs this energy the image he has created to represent his desires takes on a physical reality in the material world. The practice of magic is designed to sidetrack the conscious mind which is conditioned by preconceived ideas and contact the subconscious which is the key to producing magical results.

Due to the finding of modern psychology we know that each of us operates on at least three mental levels. These are defined as the subconscious, the conscious and the superconscious. The conscious mind speaks for itself for it is the level of physical awareness experienced during our waking hours in which we operate as normal human beings.

The subconscious is the twilight world of our dreams, fantasies, hopes and fears. Under normal circumstances the subconscious operates only during our sleeping period when the physical functions of our bodies are reduced to a minimum. This mental state is characterised by dreams, visions and nightmares as we digest the day's events but it is also the receiver of images and symbols arising from what is often called the spiritual realm.

The superconsciousness, or higher self, acts whether we are asleep or awake to integrate the other two mental states. A breakdown in the role of the superconscious leads to the degeneration of the mental faculties described by modern psychiatry as mental illness. In practical magic the subconscious is trained to act as a radio receiver which can communicate with other realms in order to produce magical results on the physical plane.

Before moving on to the preparations for magical working it should be clearly understood that the practice of magic to obtain material benefits is the final resort and should be used only when all other options have been exhausted. The magical adept learns not to covet material possessions but to use them while he is incarnated on the physical level. Fanatical craving for wealth or material things is a spiritual sickness but there is no reason why we should feel guilty about wanting to live in comfortable conditions while on Earth. There is very little spiritual virtue in being a beggar despite what some religions may teach. In practice you will usually find that the genuine magician or occultist leads a simple life as a matter of personal choice.

Another point to remember is that there is no point in performing a complex ritual to get a new car and then sitting back and waiting for the local garage to deliver the latest model to your door. Participation is the key word in any form of magical endeavour. You will always be expected to initiate activity on the physical plane to make your magic work but the powers-that-be will do the rest once you have made the initial move.

Natural and life forces

One final very important point before we move on to some practical work. There is obviously a spiritual dimension to magic. In this book you will find many references to the gods and goddesses of classical mythology, to nature spirits and archangels. Religion is an attempt by humankind to classify Divinity in a way which the majority can understand. The purpose of the gods is to bring the unknowable down to human scale — to reduce the macrocosm to the microcosm without losing its divine nature. In practice the Old Gods were personifications of natural forces and aspects of the life force — the creative energy which flows through the universe.

These various aspects of the life force have been visually represented by different races and cultures by the use of what are called archetypal images. In many cases human heroes and heroines who acted as civilising influences in the early stages of humanity's history were transformed into gods or semi-divine being after they died. Some examples are Isis and Osiris in ancient Egypt, Odin in Northern Europe, Oanes in Babylon, and the founders of Buddhism and Christianity.

A magician can be a witch, pagan, Christian, Moslem, Hindu, Buddhist, Jew, Taoist or a Shinto; for all these religious beliefs have their own magical traditions. It is also possible for a magician to follow none of these religions. One word of warning if you decide to invoke gods or spiritual beings in your magical rituals: never mix different religious systems. It will become obvious as we progress through this book that gods and goddesses from different cultures have identical characteristics. However, if you do a ritual for wisdom and invoke Thoth, Hermes and Odin in the same breadth do not be surprised if your magical wires get crossed. In practice if a magician wishes to introduce a religious element into his magical rituals he will choose one which corresponds to his present cultural background or past life experience and stay with that system exclusively.

Preparation and relaxation

Before setting out on the magical path some preliminary work is required. As with anything we try to achieve in life the correct preparation is essential if success is to be the end result. The highly competitive, hustle-bustle lives the majority of us live today can create tension, physical debility and a general feeling of irritability. Such negative feelings are not conducive to the practice of magic.

The magician must learn to relax and open his mind to the force; he must learn to flow with its positive energy. You cannot perform magic properly if your mind is buzzing with the undigested events of the day or negative thoughts about how you are going to pay next month's mortgage. You need to be relaxed and self-assured.

There are several techniques available to attain this state of relaxation. The easiest to perform are the following two exercises. As with all the practical exercises in this book it is recommended that you read them through carefully several times so they are fully understood before proceeding. For the first exercise select a room in the house where you will not be disturbed for at least 30 minutes to carry out the two exercises properly. Hang up the telephone and lock the door if there is any chance you will be interrupted.

Sit in a comfortable chair but one which provides adequate support to keep your back straight. Your feet should be placed flat on the floor, knees together and hands laid flat palms downward on the top of your thighs. This posture is known as the Egyptian meditation position and is depicted in the paintings on the walls of ancient tombs. It is more physically comfortable than the usual crosslegged lotus position used in Eastern meditation and yoga. Loose clothing should be worn and the room should be warm but well ventilated. A hot, stuffy room will encourage sleep not relaxation. At the end of this exercise you should be in a relaxed but alert state not half asleep.

Commence your first relaxation exercise as follows. Visualize in your mind's eye a ball of white light about the size of a tennis ball hovering above the crown of your head. Imagine this ball of light entering your head. It is now slowly moving down through your head. When it reaches your throat the ball of light moves to the right, travelling across your right shoulder and down your right arm. When it reaches the fingertips of your right hand it pauses and then travels back up your arm, across your right shoulder and rests at the centre of your throat.

Imagine the ball of white light is moving again, travelling across your left shoulder and down your left arm to the fingers of your left hand. It pauses there for a few seconds and then travels back up your left arm, across your left shoulder to rest in the centre of your throat where it began.

From this position visualize the ball of light travelling down the centre of your body to rest at your solar plexus. From that position imagine the ball of white light travelling down your left leg, pausing when it reaches your toes and then returning to its original position.

16

Repeat this procedure with your right leg, the ball of light coming back to rest at the centre of your abdomen.

When this has been completed imagine the ball of white light returning up your body from the solar plexus to the centre of your throat. The ball of light pauses there and then travels up to the crown of your head. There it emerges and hovers some six inches above your head. In your mind's eye imagine the ball of white light gradually fading into nothingness.

With the completion of the first stage of the relaxation process we shall now move on to the second relaxation exercise. Still sitting upright in your chair, begin to concentrate on your feet. Tense and then relax your feet. Feel the tension flowing out of the muscles and any tiredness evaporating. Slowly move up your body, tensing and then relaxing your legs, abdomen, chest, arms and neck. Experience the tension going out of your face, feel the muscles relax and draining off tension.

It is essential that you concentrate on each part of your body as you perform this second exercise. If you let your mind wander and discover other mundane thoughts to think about stop the exercise immediately and begin again at your feet.

If you do these simple exercises properly then you will become completely relaxed.

This state should not be confused with the tiredness you experience just before going to bed at the end of a hard day's work which people sometimes regard as being relaxed. After doing these exercises you should be feeling alert, full of energy but free from tension and worries about mundane matters. Although these exercises are provided as a method of achieving the right state of mind for magical working they can also be used to relax after a period of intense pressure or physical exertion.

Breathing

Correct breathing is an essential aspect of any form of meditation or relaxation. Most of us think that breathing is such a natural action that we must be doing it correctly all the time. Ask any athlete or opera singer about breathing correctly and you will find out that there is more to it than one supposes.

Breathing is nature's way of providing enough oxygen to the

brain, the heart and the blood to keep the human body working. If the amount of oxygen supplied to the brain, for instance, is increased or decreased dramatically physical reactions will occur, ranging from the unpleasant to the potentially lethal. When we are excited, tense, anxious or emotionally disturbed our breathing rate increases. For people suffering from hypertension and anxiety this can result in palpitations or attacks of hysteria. In order to help the relaxation process, regulate your breathing pattern to a slightly lower rate than usual during the exercise.

Breathe in to a rhythm of 1-2-3 and breathe out to a rhythm of 1-2-3-4. At first you will have to force yourself to make a conscious effort to regulate your breathing in this way. After a while, once you have instructed your mind to do it, this type of deep breathing will become second nature. The breathing pattern recommended is quite safe and will be beneficial to your physical and mental well-being and preparedness for magical working.

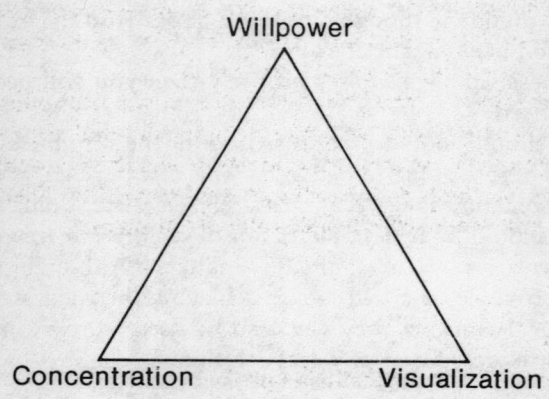

1   The magical triangle.

The magical triangle

Having learnt the philosophy behind magic and how to relax the next stage is understanding how the magical art works. The key to practical magic can be revealed in the simple symbol known as the magical triangle. You can draw this on a piece of plain white paper with a pencil, crayon or felt-tip pen. At the top of the triangle write the word will-power. At the bottom left-hand corner write concentration. Finally, at the bottom right-hand corner write visualization (see Figure 1). The magical triangle represents the three prime qualities you must acquire or develop in order to work magic. They are imagined in the form of a triangle because although each is separate they are linked with each other.

Willpower

The first quality, that of willpower, has already been touched upon. In the earlier definition of magic it was said to be the art of causing changes in accordance with the *will* of the individual. You must believe in yourself as a person to practice magic. The relaxation exercises, if performed properly, will help to make you a more positive and assured person; someone who is not the victim of the capricious tides of destiny but who knows what he wants from this incarnation and is willing to go out and get it.

It should be obvious that this does not mean trampling on everyone else on the way to achieving what you want. One very important thing magic, or any other form of occult development, teaches us is that service to others is the greatest goal in life. There is a great difference between self-confidence and ego-mania.

Concentration

The second point of the magical triangle is concentration. As with the relaxation exercise, it is essential in magical workings to concentrate on what you are doing at the time to the exclusion of everthing else around you. All other distractions should be ignored and the mind must be focused on the particular action being carried out and the desired end result.

Today we are faced with so many distractions and conflicting visual images, sounds and experiences in our daily lives that many people find it very difficult to concentrate on just one thing or action. Meditation can be a useful tool to increase the power of concentration. In practice meditation is an advanced form of relaxation. Before meditating it would be advisable to perform the relaxation exercises. In the meditative technique outlined below the mind is focused on one object, symbol or image to the exclusion of everything else.

The choice of a meditation symbol is a personal one. It is better to choose something which is abstract or mundane rather than something with private or emotional associations. A flower, a stone or the photograph of a landscape you have never visited is ideal. For the purpose of this exercise we have selected a lighted candle. Sit in the Egyptian meditation position as previously described. If necessary perform the two relaxation exercises so you are in the correct state of mind.

Place the lighted candle in a suitable safe holder about three feet in front of you and make sure that the candle is the only object within your range of vision as you look at it. Place it on a table, for instance, but well away from other small objects. Ensure you can sit looking at the candle without feeling any discomfort. All other lights in the room should be extinguished before you commence this exercise.

Light the candle as a deliberate act. Concentrate on the striking of the match, observe the flame of the match blazing and watch as it ignites the candle.

Returning to your meditation position, concentrate on the candle flame using it as the focus of your attention. Use the breath control method previously explained. Banish all other thoughts from your mind. As far as you are concerned nothing else but the candle flame exists in the world. The room around you has faded away and there is just the candle flame and you.

It is essential that when performing this concentration exercise you do not suffer any physical strain. Blink normally and do not overstrain your eyes. Stop immediately if your eyes start to water or ache. At first do this exercise for short periods, perhaps five minutes per day, and work up gradually to thirty minutes after a week or two's practice. With the relaxation exercises this totals 60 minutes of practical work which even the busiest person should be able to fit in to his daily schedule. Once you have learnt to concentrate the exercise described will no longer be required. The relaxation exercises can also be reduced or used only when some benefit is required or prior to a magical working.

Visualization

The last point of the magical triangle is visualization which is directly linked to the other qualities required by the would-be magician. It is essential that you should be able to build up mental images with intense clarity. To a greater or lesser extent we are all victims of day-dreams. Usually at the least convenient moment in the day visual images pour into our minds and we become so engrossed in our inner reveries that the world around us ceases to exist. The creation of magical images can be described quite accurately as lucid day-dreaming under controlled conditions with a definite purpose in mind.

There are several techniques for improving the power of visualization. One proven method is to draw a circle in black on a piece of white paper or card and divide it into equal segments. Colour alternate quarters, using a thick black felt pen or crayon, and leave the other segments uncoloured. As in the meditation exercise with the candle, concentrate on this black and white image for a few minutes. Then close your eyes and visualize it in your imagination. Because of the two-colour design of the circle it should appear easily in your mind's eye. This exercise will help your natural ability to visualize, which we all possess, to increase.

A second method is one used in the training of secret agents who must be expert observers. Ask a friend to select a number of small everyday articles used in the home without you seeing them. These are placed on a tray and covered in a cloth. The helper places the tray in front of you and removes the cloth for a period of 60 seconds only before replacing it. During the time the tray is uncovered look at each object in turn, note their position, colour, shape, size and texture.

The second person then hands you writing materials once the tray has been recovered. Note down as many items as you can remember and their exact position on the tray. To remember this information you should visualize the tray as it was when the cloth was removed.

Another exercise to tone up your visualization powers is to sit in a room which you use quite frequently. Close your eyes and imagine what the room looks like. Imagine every detail, including the texture of the carpet, the colours of the walls and furnishings, and the various objects in it. If you can, try to imagine the characteristic smells which any room used for daily living acquires. Another mental exercise is to imagine a fresh red rose hovering in front of you. Visualize its petals covered in early morning dew, feel the texture of its stem with thorns attached and the subtle fragrance of its perfume.

The purpose of all these exercises is to strengthen your imagination. Later on in this book, when we come to the practical magical rituals, this ability to create strong visual images will be seen as an essential part of practising magic. If you want the desired result to your magical effort you must be capable of visualizing the goal and making it happen as if you were watching the event on a movie screen. This is applicable not only to material requirements, like finding a new job or house, but also to healing the sick which can be achieved in a magical context. If you are going to use the force to attract both material and spiritual benefits you must be an expert in visualization techniques.

By building up in your mind an image of what you want to achieve you are producing an astral blueprint of the reality which will manifest as a result of your hard work. Every architect's dream house, every writer's best seller and every painter's Old Master began in the imagination. The ritual which follows the act of mental creation is the method used to concentrate the power raised by the magician and project it into the ether.

In addition to increasing your powers of creative imagination it is also recommended that you heighten your normal sensory perceptions. You can do this quite easily by collecting a range of objects made from different materials such as wood, silk, plastic, metal, velvet, wool, cloth, etc. Close your eyes and at random feel each of these objects in turn, experiencing their unique texture. A similar exercise can be carried out using a range of different perfumes. Hearing can also be sharpened by sitting in a garden, closing your eyes and listening to the wide spectrum of sounds. Under normal circumstances this background noise is hardly noticed but with eyes closed and the mind concentrated on the sounds it is amazing what you can hear.

The three sides of the magical triangle are linked. Taken together will-power, visualization and concentration are the three most important aspects of magical training. You must have faith in yourself and the positive attitude that your magic will work. You must possess the ability to concentrate exclusively on one thing, object or goal. Finally, having decided on your aim, you must have the power of the creative imagination to visualize the magical working coming to fruition on the physical plane.

Earlier we mentioned the Hermetic axiom 'As above, so below' which is crystallised in the theory of magical correspondences. A list of these is given at the end of this book and it should be studied carefully. The list is divided into two sections for elemental magic and planetary magic. In later chapters of this book the significance of these correspondences will be discussed. Each element and planet is associated with different qualities and rulership over a particular aspect of human life. These correspondences have obvious connections with astrology which originated as a religious belief with magical overtones.

In practical magic by using the colours, metals, symbols and images relating to a particular energy force you can tune in to that influence and attract to you the qualities it represents. The use of magical correspondences is equivalent to programming a computer with the correct data so it will produce the right answer.

Symbolism

Symbolism is another aspect of magic which should be studied. When a simple magical ritual is being performed the subconscious mind is being used. Although the conscious mind responds to the written or spoken word, the subconscious reacts best to visual images or symbols. These symbols act as a form of shorthand which relays to the subconscious mind information which the magician wishes it to know in order to achieve the result of his ritual or working.

The use of symbols as a magical shorthand can be illustrated by the planetary sigils used by astrologers to produce horoscopes. Although such symbols obviously have an esoteric use they can also be utilised as a method of imparting spiritual information in a simple and concise form. In the magical sense the five elemental forces of

Fire, Earth, Air, Water and Spirit can be represented in symbolic form in the drawing of a pentagram or five-pointed star.

One way to contact the subconscious in magical practice is to translate words or letters into symbols. For example, if you want to perform a magical working to pass an examination, you take the key phrase 'I will pass my exam' and break it down to the initial letters IWPME. An ideogram is then constructed from these to represent the key phrase and therefore the essence of the wish (see Figure 2). This symbol can be used as a meditation sigil which will be registered in the subconscious mind and bring about the desired result.

Preparation

The preparation for any magical work is very important. Ideally a separate room should be kept for your relaxation/meditation exercises and magical rituals. This may not be possible within the confines of modern living but is desirable. If you cannot have a room exclusively for this use all the time then use the same room each time.

The purpose of a separate room is not for secrecy but for the commonsense reason that it will provide essential privacy, freedom from outside distractions, as well as peace and quiet. You do not want your next-door neighbour or another member of the family who is not involved in your magical activities wandering in when you are in the middle of a meditation exercise or ritual.

As you develop on the magical path you will find that you will be able to work magic in the most unlikely places. An advanced magician using creative imagination should be able to perform a 'ritual' entirely on the mental level even on a crowded train on the way home from work. It is however some time before the aspiring magician reaches that degree of expertise. You will, therefore, need to rely on a suitable peaceful home environment for a little while. Most of the magic described in this book can be practised with the minimum of equipment quite easily in any room of the house.

If you can spare a separate room in your house and wish to set aside a working space for your occult studies then it should be prepared properly before commencing any practical exercises. A

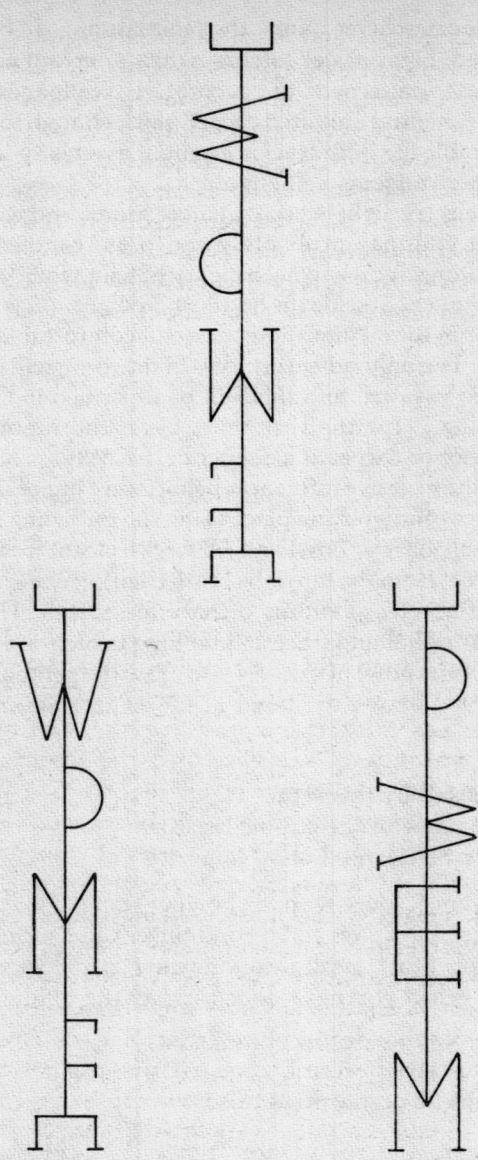

2 Symbolic ideogram: I will pass my exam–IWPME.

neutral colour scheme and the minimum of furnishings is recommended. Light pastel colours, white or cream are best for the walls because patterned or decorative wallpapers can be a distraction. A neutral coloured carpet, thick enough to deaden noise and comfortable for bare feet, is essential especially if you are in a flat with other residents below you.

A central electric light is usual in most rooms and will be required even though you may probably want to use candles during your magical workings. You will need plenty of light when you are setting up your equipment outside the hours of daylight. As you will also be using this room for meditation exercises a comfortable chair should be provided. The only other furniture in the room will be the altar, if you decide to use one, and this will be described in Chapter 2.

Before using it for the first time, clean the room thoroughly. Sweep the floor or carpet as a deliberate act. While you are doing so visualise all the negative influences being swept out of the room. You can then bless your working place using the following simple ritual.

Take a small glass or bowl and fill it with clean, fresh water. This can come direct from the tap or be bottled spring water. In a separate bowl place three teaspoonfuls of natural sea salt. Using the first finger of your right hand trace an invoking pentagram (see Figure 3) in the air over the bowl of salt. As you draw the pentagram, imagine it being formed above the bowl in blue light. Say the following words:

I bless this salt by this sign
and in the name of the cosmic creator
that it may be cleansed of all impurity

Repeat this procedure with the bowl of water. Take three pinches of salt between your first and second fingers and sprinkle it into the bowl of water. Stir the salt into the water in a clockwise direction three times. When you have done this say the following words:

Water and salt purify the body and
the spirit
With them I bless this room

Walk around the room three times in a clockwise direction sprinkling the mixture of water and salt. At the compass points of West, North, East and South pause for a few seconds and raise the

26

bowl in salute. As you walk around the room imagine that it is becoming filled with brilliant white light. Return to your original position and meditate for a few minutes on the purpose of the room and the magical work you intend to perform within it. This blessing ritual, like most magical acts, is simple but effective. Your room has now been cleansed on both a material and psychic/spiritual level and is ready for use.

Newcomers to the magical path are often intimidated by the ritual aspect of the subject. In fact the use of ritual is only a disciplining structure used to aid concentration and provide the right state of mind for magic. A ritual does not have to be a theatrical performance with a long script to learn like a grand opera. The simpler it is the more likely it will be that results are obtained. If you are worrying about trying to remember a lot of flowery words or flamboyant actions then your energies are being diverted from the true purpose of the ritual. This is not to say that there are times when such rituals have their purpose but this is not usually in the context of really practical magic.

Rituals

As you progress the ability to construct suitable rituals for all purposes will develop. Remember the following golden rules when improvising any ritual. Always have a beginning, a middle and an end planned. Do not just make it up as you go along unless you are very experienced. To mark the beginning you can make a simple declaration of the intent of the ritual such as 'This ritual is to send healing to my friend Linda who is suffering from tension'. The middle part of the ritual should be the actual healing with petitions to the ruling archangel or god/goddess and the actual projection of the healing energy. When the ritual has been completed simply say firmly 'The ritual is ended' before closing your circle.

It is a good idea when the ritual is ended and you have cleared away everything to have a small meal to 'earth' yourself. This does not have to be a five-course gourmet dinner. A cheese sandwich and a cup of tea will suffice. Before commencing any ritual it is recommended that you do not eat for at least three hours. Some magicians abstain from sexual activity for 24 hours before any important ritual. Heavy food tends to interfere with magical workings for it makes you feel mentally sluggish and physically tired. The outlet of sexual energy depletes the life force so pre-magical celibacy makes good sense.

In the blessing ritual the acknowledgement of the four quarters or compass points was mentioned. The symbolism of the magical circle is a very important subject in occult literature. Depending on what literature you read or which magical practitioner you speak to, the significance of the circle will be explained in one of two ways. A magician will say it is a protective measure designed to keep out negative influences, whereas a practising witch will tell you it is used to keep the physic power raised during magical rituals from escaping.

Both these explanations are valid but the real reason for a circle is to create a separate working space within the temple or room you are using for magical rituals. It is another method used by the magician to create a suitable atmosphere. Ideally, a separate room should be set aside for your occult work but the raising of a magical circle creates a temporary temple.

Old books on magic and popular occult thrillers depict the magician drawing a circle in coloured chalks on the floor. Unless you really want to roll back the carpet every time you do a ritual this is a time-consuming and unnecessary exercise. The magical circle can be created just as effectively on the inner or mental level. If you are working out of doors then the circle can be cut in the earth with your magical sword (see Chapter 2) if required.

The magical circle is divided into four quarters or segments. Each of these is assigned to one of the compass points and one of the four elements. Each one is also under the rulership of one of the lords of the elements or 'Mighty Ones'. (Further information on these elemental guardians is given in Chapter 6.)

Before each magical working the circle is raised and at the end is closed down. The ritual for doing this is as follows. You will need a compass to find the cardinal points, West, North, South, East as well as a small bell, water and salt. Fill your chalice (See Chapter 2) with blessed water using the procedure given earlier in this chapter. Beginning at the West, walk deosil (clockwise) around the circle sprinkling the water. Then beginning in the North, hold the pentacle in front of you and carry it around the circle. Beginning in the East walk around the circle with a lighted incense-burner. Finally, beginning in the South, walk around the circle with a lighted candle.

Walk to the centre of the circle and meditate on the four elemental forces (see Chapter 6 and list of magical correspondences). Go to the North quarter and, using either a sword or the wand, walk around the circle deosil, symbolically 'cutting' or tracing the actual magical circle. As you do this visualize a ring of small blue flames springing up where you are pointing the magical tool.

When the circle is complete return to the North quarter and invoke the elemental lord. You do this by 'drawing' an invoking pentagram (see Figure 3) in the air using the sword or wand. When you draw this symbol hold your arm out stiffly and perform the action with firm and definite strokes. Always begin at the top of the figure and end with a downward movement as indicated in the diagram. As you draw the pentagram imagine it glowing in front of you, outlined in blue light. Say the following words:

O great Lord of the North and
the elemental power of Earth
I invoke your presence to
protect this circle during
the ritual I am about to perform.

Ring the bell three times. Then walk deosil to the other quarters repeating the above words but substituting 'Lord of the East/South/West' and 'the elemental power of Air/Fire/Water' as appropriate.

When the ritual is ended close down by walking northways or anti-clockwise around the circle. At each of the quarters beginning in the North and ending in the West say the following words.

O great Lord of the North/East/South/West
and elemental power of the Earth/Air/Fire/Water
I thank you for your protection during this ritual and dismiss you
in this sign.

Draw a banishing pentagram, as shown in Figure 3, then extinguish all the candles.

In erecting this magical circle we have begun in each case in the North quarter. This is a traditional sacred point in the Western

29

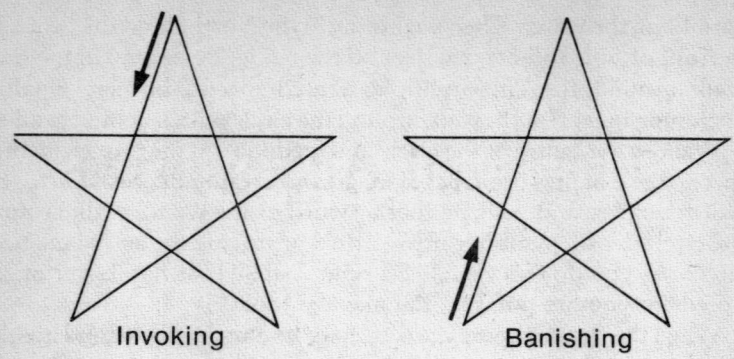

3 Invoking and banishing pentagrams.

magical tradition. It is the direction of the Pole Star, the realm of the gods and the cosmic Tree of Life. Some magicians begin in the East, which is the direction of the rising Sun, a symbol of the life force, and is just as valid.

2 Ritual Accessories

If you examine the Tarot card known as The Magician (Figure 4) you will see that he holds in his right hand an upraised wand while his left hand points downwards. On the table or altar is laid a sword, a chalice and a disc which has a pentagram or five-pointed star inscribed on it. The position of the magician with one hand upraised and the other pointed down is a symbolic gesture illustrating the Hermetic axiom 'As above, so below'. It also indicates that the magician is drawing down power from above for he is not the source of the power but a channel which it uses.

The magician is wearing a simple robe and around his waist is a belt in the form of a serpent with its tail in its mouth – a very ancient symbol of eternity and the life force. The Tarot card depicts the archetypal magician who, on the highest level, can be identified with the dieties of magical wisdom such as Thoth, the ibis-headed god of ancient Egypt, Odin, the hooded shaman god of Northern Europe, or Hermes, the androgynous god of Greece.

The magician's tools

In both elemental and planetary magic the use of the four working tools of the magician are emphasised. These are the wand, chalice, sword and pentacle (see Figure 5). In our introduction we referred to the ancient beginnings of magic among the cave shamans of the prehistoric Stone Age. It has been suggested that the four magical tools originated during this period. They were the everyday weapons used by the early hunters to capture and kill their quarry.

In their most basic form they were the dagger (sword), the club (wand), the shield (pentacle) and the hunting horn (chalice).

As religious awareness grew these weapons would have taken on a more symbolic or sacred meaning. At first they were associated with the Horned God, who was the Lord of the Wild Hunt, and then they became identified with the use of magic for various purposes. The four magical tools received their most sophisticated interpretation in ancient Celtic mythology. Everyone knows of the magical sword Excalibur given to King Arthur by the Lady of the Lake. In the earliest stories of the Holy Grail it is not a Christian symbol but a magical cauldron of inspiration, rebirth and fertility. In the Irish myths the god Dagda carried a huge club which was the prototype of the magical wand.

The ownership and use of a set of magical working tools is not a *sine qua non* for travelling on the magical path, although those magicians who follow traditions which revel in theatricals will argue otherwise. The magical tools represent aspects of the magician's personality and inner self which he is projecting into the outer world. In common with the weapons of the hunter or the medieval knight, they provide a clear indication to those around him of what he stands for and represents.

Magical tools are symbolic extensions of the magician's own will and identity but they can be dispensed with once the magician has sufficient knowledge to operate without them. Until that time they serve their purpose. Experienced magicians may not need either working tools or ritual (in the accepted sense) at all. The novice, however, will find these 'theatrical props' useful until such time as he has gained mastery over both himself and the forces he will be invoking in his operations.

The symbolism of the magical tools can be interpreted on several levels. On a purely mundane level, reverting back to the weapons of the prehistoric hunter, they represent the four essentials required by a human being to survive in the material world – air (the wand), water (the chalice), light/heat (the sword) and food (the pentacle).

This very basic interpretation of the working tools reinforces the old occult belief that although humans are spiritual beings they are incarnated on the material plane in physical bodies. Asceticism and the rejection of the natural world for a spiritual Utopia has never been a philosophy widely accepted by magicians in the West or

4 The Magician (from the Waite Tarot deck).

indeed genuine Eastern practitioners of magic. We are given bodily form in this world but, by denying its reality, hinder our own spiritual progress. Abstinence is a feature of some magical work but only for a limited period and for specific reasons.

On an occult (hidden) level the magical tools represent the four elemental powers or forces which medieval philosophers believed were the foundation of the universe – Fire, Earth, Air and Water. We will be examining the wider implications of this in our chapter on elemental magic. Here we will examine their relevance to the working tools of the practising magus. The elemental forces are attributed to the working tools as follows:

Wand – Air – Wisdom
Sword – Fire – Will-power
Chalice – Water – Perception
Pentacle – Earth – Knowledge

It should be pointed out that some practitioners of magic attribute the wand to fire and the sword to air. This attribution seems to date from the rituals practised by the Hermetic Order of the Golden Dawn which flourished in Victorian times. In this book the wand has been attributed to Air because this is what we were taught and it seems to make symbolic sense. The exchanging of the symbolic attributions does not seem to have any adverse effect on magical efficiency for those magicians who reverse the above attributes so it is up to the reader to make the decision which suits individual feelings about this matter.

We will now examine the symbolism of each of the four magical tools in turn and their use in practical magic.

The wand

In practice the wand or staff is the primary working tool of the magician. It represents his rod of power through which is concentrated the mind stuff that makes magic work. In ancient times the wand was the sceptre or staff of office carried by a king or queen to show that they possessed the divine authority of the gods as their representatives on Earth.

The wand represents the element of Air which is symbolic of the mind, the intellect and communication. In the zodiac the Air element

34

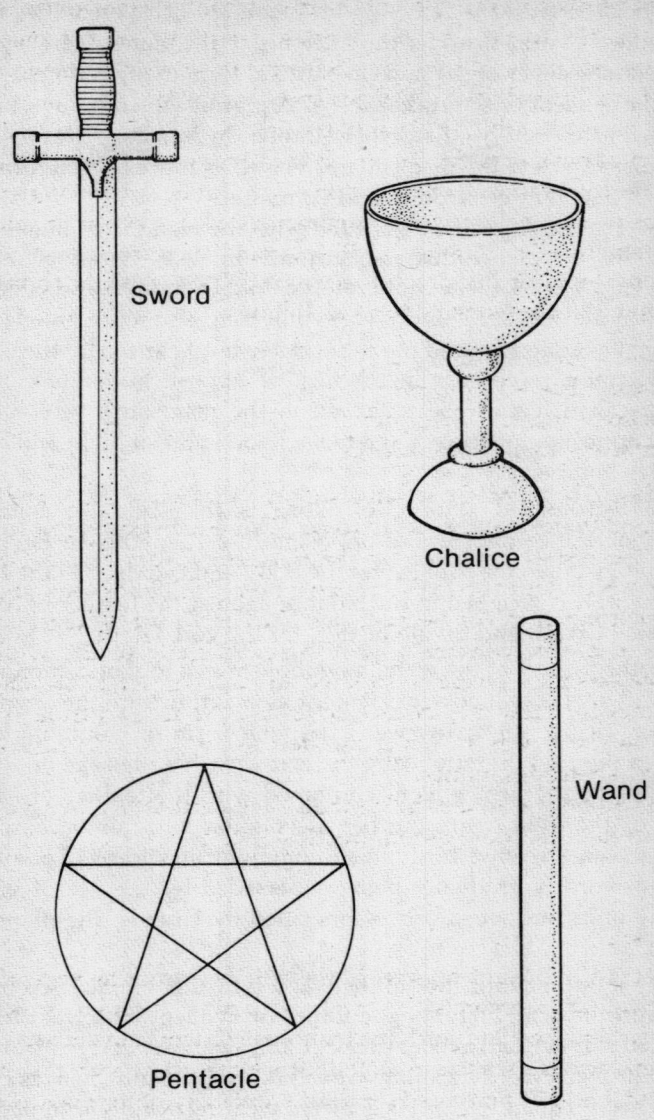

Sword

Chalice

Wand

Pentacle

5 **The magical tools.**

is associated with the Sun sign of Gemini which personifies these attributes. Gemini is under the rulership of the planet Mercury, the winged messenger of the gods in classical Roman mythology. Air is also the element of the zodiacal sign Aquarius which is governed in modern astrology by the planet Uranus. In astrology Uranus also has rulership over the magical arts as well as more hi-tech forms of wizardry such as electronics and computers.

The triad of Air signs associated with the wand is completed by Libra. At first glance this association is unclear. However, in the Tarot card The Magician holds aloft a double-ended wand which he grasps in the middle. This double symbolism, also represented in the two snakes coiled around the caduceus (wand) carried by the Greek god Hermes, represents the duality of opposites manifest in the universe which must be balanced in the magician's personality. These opposites are male and female, good and evil, light and dark, positive and negative, etc.

The astrological symbol of Libra is the scales or balance, signifying the equilibrium of opposing forces. In ancient Egyptian mythology when the soul leaves the body and is judged in the Halls of Amenti it is weighed in the balance against the feather of Maat, goddess of truth and divine justice, by the god Thoth.

Another aspect of the wand's symbolism as a tool of communication and intellectual power is its past association with the arrow. A message tied to an arrow was a popular form of communicating news in the past. Symbolically the arrow with a message on it was replaced by the pen (which, combined with the feather of Maat, gives us the quill pen); another association with air because the feather comes from a bird which communicates ideas. Today the written word is gradually being superseded by the use of visual display units and word processors ruled by Uranus, the planet of magic.

The esoteric significance of the wand is further emphasised by its link with the Scandinavian god Odin, or Woden, who was always depicted carrying a traveller's staff. Odin's name is derived from an Indo-European word meaning wind and, traditionally, he was a god of storms. Frequently Odin is depicted wearing a wide-brimmed hat and carrying a staff, two items of dress associated with Mercury and Hermes. To many ancient peoples the power of the wind was associated with spiritual energy and the life force. Odin was also the god who invented the Runic alphabet, having gained the wisdom of the runes by hanging on the Cosmic Tree for nine days and nights.

If possible the magician should attempt to make his own wand. The wood to be used should be cut when the Moon is waning so as little damage as possible is done to the tree. Before cutting the wood always ask permission to take it from the tree and bury a silver-coloured coin among the roots as a symbolic offering to the tree spirit. The traditional magician's wand is usually made of hazel and is cut from the tree at Sunrise. Opinions differ as to the length of the wand but it should really be no longer than the measurement from the user's elbow joint to his fingertips although ceremonial staves can, of course, be much longer.

One tip of the wand can be shaped to a point while the opposite end is forked, thus representing the male and female principles. Alternatively the wand can be hollowed out and a magnetised steel rod or seven pieces of metal representing the planetary forces (see list of magical correspondences) inserted inside it. The wand can either be painted (yellow is the traditional colour of Air), left plain or stained with a natural wood finish.

The chalice

The chalice is the second magical tool on The Magician's altar on the Tarot card. It is a feminine symbol representing the element Water. In ancient times it was the cauldron of divine inspiration, rebirth and fertility of the Celtic Moon goddess Ceridwen. The cup, cauldron or bowl symbolises the womb of the Great Mother Goddess (nature) from which all things are born and to which all things return at death.

At the beginning of time the planets and stars were formed in the stellar womb of outer space, and in primordial times life on Earth originated in the oceans. In occult symbolism the chalice is associated with the Moon, darkness, the sea, night, underground caves and intergalactic space.

Originally the chalice was the hunting horn of the cave shaman. It was a symbol of both the male and female cosmic energies flowing through the universe. Today the chalice is exclusively a female symbol, although in the ritual symbolism of plunging the sword or wand into it this is transformed into the uniting of opposites.

37

One form of the horn is the cornucopia, symbol of the Roman goddess Fortuna, which overflowed with fruits, grains and flowers. She was the original Lady Luck invoked by modern gamblers. In Celtic times the cauldron was used for sacrificial purposes and this symbolism survives in the communion chalice of the Catholic Mass.

Although the chalice is regarded as a symbol of feminine passivity, sensitivity and negativity, it is very powerful on the magical level. The wand and the sword may represent masculine symbols of the life force but the chalice (with the pentacle) symbolizes the subtle feminine principle which is sometimes undervalued by magicians because it works in less obvious ways. They do so at their cost, though, because the power of the feminine principle is a very potent force and one of the foundations of true magic.

The chalice has several uses in magical rituals. It is used to hold the consecrated water and salt employed to bless the temple and cast the circle. It can also be used to hold wine when a libation is called for during a ritual.

Traditionally the chalice should be made of silver, the planetary metal of the Moon and the Great Goddess. If silver is too expensive for your pocket, glass, wood or pottery can be safely used. The chalice should be kept as plain as possible as highly stylised or decorated cups on the altar are a distraction. If required, a simple crescent Moon could be engraved on the chalice as a symbolic decoration.

The sword

Historically, swords are a late development in weapons of warfare. The oldest swords date from the Bronze Age and were a larger version of the dagger or knife which had been in use for thousands of years. The sword in magical symbolism is associated with the elemental force of Fire, which is a symbol of cosmic power and inner strength because a sword is forged from iron or steel under extreme heat by a blacksmith.

In ancient mythology the pantheon of deities often included a divine blacksmith who made the weapons for the Old Gods. Two examples of these blacksmith gods are the Roman god of fire, Vulcan, and Wayland the Smith who made the weapons for the

Norse gods. The sword is under the rulership of the Archangel Michael in planetary magic (see Chapter 7), the planet Mars and the Sun, the elemental colour of red and the zodiacal signs Aries, Leo and Sagittarius.

In the Middle Ages it was expected that any competent magician would make his own sword. Today, when sword-making skills are not so common, it is permitted to purchase a sword for magical use. Old swords can be bought in antique shops but unless they have only been used for ceremonial or decorative purposes such weapons may have unpleasant vibrations. To be on the safe side it is recommended that if you cannot manufacture your own sword you purchase a brand new one from a reputable occult supplier.

In occult lore the sword is associated with will-power, strength and the male aspect of the life force. In medieval times the sword was used to delineate the magical circle and to command and banish any spirits which might materialise in it. Today we have a more enlightened view of magic and the invocation of magical energies but the sword still has an important role to play. As an alternative to the wand it can be used to 'cut' the circle and to direct magical energy.

In the ancient legends of King Arthur the young warrior was unable to begin his quest to found the Fellowship of the Round Table until he had received his magical sword Excalibur. The attaining of the sword by the aspiring magician symbolises the moment when he can take his first practical steps on the magical path.

The pentacle

The pentacle (pantacle) is the last of the four magical working tools which can be seen on the altar in the Tarot card known as The Magician. It is associated with the elemental power of Earth, the feminine principle in its aspect as the Great Mother and the zodiacal signs Taurus, Virgo and Capricorn. On a mundane level the pentacle represents materialism but it also has a deeper symbolism for it represents the Earth plane in which all souls are incarnated to learn the lessons of life.

Some religions emphasize the spiritual to such an extent that the material world is rejected as an illusion or temptation which must be ignored if true progress is to be made. In magic the physical plane is seen as the reflection of the spiritual reality which exists behind outer appearances. Matter and spirit are regarded by the magician as complementary aspects of the same primal reality; if we reject one then we are cutting ourselves off from the other. Only by deeply experiencing the material and spiritual worlds can the personality develop and mature correctly.

The pentacle, like the chalice, is a symbol of the feminine principle. In ancient times it was universally believed that the Earth was represented by a goddess and this led to the feminine descriptions of Mother Earth and Mother Nature used to describe the natural world. Today, with increased ecological awareness of our relationship with the physical environment, the concept of the Earth as a living organism has been revived in a scientific form in accordance with modern beliefs. The scientists who have reformulated this old idea have even named the Earth entity Gaia, from the Great Mother Goddess in Greek mythology.

In its original form the pentacle was the shield of the ancient hunter and was viewed purely as a defensive weapon. Symbolically, and remember that symbolism is the language of magic, it is not a weapon of war but one of peace. In magical work there are times when we need to shield ourselves from negative influences, so the pentacle is therefore a symbol of psychic protection. It can also be used in healing rituals to project energy because, like the magical circle, the pentacle is round. The sacred circle, either with a dot or an equal-armed cross at its centre, is a very powerful symbol representing wholeness and the unity of creation.

Making a pentacle is fairly simple. It can be made from wood, metal, stone or pottery and should be between four and six inches in diameter. On one side of the pentacle should be carved, engraved or painted a pentagram or five-pointed star.

Once you have made or collected a set of four magical tools they will have to be consecrated before they can be used in practical magic. Consecration is a deliberate act where the tools are set aside only for specific use in magical workings.

For the consecration ritual choose a day when the Moon is waxing or increasing in size towards Full. Using the formula given in Chapter 1 for blessing your magical working place consecrate a bowl of water. Collect a bowl of earth from the garden and light some incense and a white candle. Sprinkle the blessed water over the chalice saying the following words:

I bless this chalice with the elemental power of Water that it may be dedicated to the Great Work and aid me in the magical art.

Repeat this procedure with the wand, pentacle and sword. Taking the bowl of earth sprinkle this over the pentacle saying:

I consecrate this pentacle with the elemental power of Earth that it may be dedicated to the Great Work and aid me in the magical art.

Repeat this procedure with the wand, sword and chalice.
Pass the wand through the incense smoke and say the following words:

I consecrate this wand with the elemental power of Air that it may be dedicated to the Great Work and aid me in the magical art.

Repeat this procedure with the sword, chalice and pentacle.
Pass the sword above the candle flame saying the following words:

I purify this sword with the elemental power of Fire that it may be dedicated to the Great Work and aid me in the magical art.

Repeat the procedure with the chalice, wand and pentacle.
As you perform these actions imagine each tool glowing with blue fire and feel them vibrating in your hands. They are being magically charged with the elemental powers of nature by this simple ritual.

When you have completed the dedication of your tools sit quietly for a few minutes meditating on their symbolism and the use to which you will put them during your magical career.

After this period of meditation wipe the tools clean, wrap them each in a black silk cloth and put them away until you are ready to use them again. They should be kept in a special box or drawer which is kept exclusively for your ritual equipment.

If you wish, on the nights of the waxing Moon you can take your tools out and place them where the Lunar rays can shine on them. This will magnetise and further charge them for magical workings.

On no account should anyone else be allowed to touch your

magical tools once they have been consecrated. If possible you should make arrangements in your will for a trusted friend to dispose of them safely after you depart to the spirit world.

Magical accessories

The robe

In addition to the four magical tools which are symbolic of the elements, the magus in the Tarot card wears a ritual robe. The wearing of a robe totally different from his ordinary clothes is a symbolic act separating the magician from the outside world. By wearing a special garment for his magical work he is signifying that it is an act apart from his normal everyday actions.

In some magical circles the robe is described as 'the garment of concealment'. When you deliberately replace your ordinary clothes with a magical robe you are making an inner statement that the hidden side of your personality is now taking control. The personality represented by your everyday clothing has been replaced by the magician who is controller of his own destiny and the weaver of occult forces. In a magical group, where several people have joined together to share rituals, the anonymous robe plays the added role of a symbol of equality. Whatever the practitioner's social position in the material world, as may be revealed by his everyday clothes, the wearing of identical magical robes proves that all are equal in the magic circle.

A magical robe is simple to make, providing you have some knowledge of dressmaking and allied skills. The usual design is either of the Arab kaftan style (patterns for which are available in high street stores) or a monk's habit. A hood which can be pulled down over the face during meditation is an optional extra.

The robe should be coloured either white or black for ordinary workings. If your finances extend to a set of different coloured robes for planetary or elemental magic then that is a good idea. Generally, most people have one robe coloured black which is an ideal colour. Garishly patterned or decorated robes, even when the decorations are magical symbols, are not recommended.

The material used to make the magical robe should be of natural origin: cotton for a light, indoor robe or wool if a magician plans to hold outdoor rituals. A cord tied around the waist is usually a good idea and the feet can be bare or encased in light slippers of a colour to match the robe.

The altar

The central point of any magical temple, as seen in The Magician Tarot card, is the altar. This obviously has religious overtones but in practice is the focal point of the magician's attention during a ritual and can be best described as the equivalent of a carpenter's bench. The four magical tools are placed on the altar, together with the censer and candles. There may also be a single light burning in a bowl to symbolize the cosmic creator or life force.

In practice the altar may simply be a small table. Traditionally, the proper magical altar is in the shape of a double cube. This symbolism is based once more on the Hermetic saying 'As above, so below' referring to the physical plane as a reflection of the spiritual realm.

The double cube is a useful form of altar to use if you have the room. It can be used as a cupboard to store your ritual accessories after use.

The altar top can be left bare or covered in a cloth of neutral colour or one of the planetary or elemental colours which can be changed for each working. Unless you cannot afford it, a simple altar cloth in black or white is the wisest choice. The selection of all the ritual equipment described in this chapter has been governed by three factors: economical consideration, possible lack of space and/or privacy and the amount of time the would-be magician can devote to his occult studies.

Incense

We have mentioned the use of incense in magical ritual. This can be purchased either from an occult shop or direct from a company specialising in supplying churches. The occult supplier will be able to offer you a wide range of custom-made magical incenses but these will cost more than if bought from a church supplier. The latter, however, will only be able to supply a limited number of incenses such as frankincense in bulk but these will be of good quality. Both suppliers will have self-igniting charcoal blocks available.

Expensive censers for burning incense ritually can be purchased. For the beginner an earthenware, heatproof bowl or dish filled with a few inches of sand will do just as well. Place the charcoal block on the sand, light one corner and wait until it is glowing hot. Then sprinkle a small amount of incense on to the block and add as required.

Record book

It is important when practising any kind of magic to be able to check the results you may obtain and also to record your progress on the path. To do this properly it is recommended that you keep a magical diary. This does not have to be elaborate, a specially purchased notebook or an adequately sized diary kept exclusively for magical use are ideal.

Into this magical record book will go all the details of your magical workings, meditations and rituals, together with the results. This record can be as concise or as wordy as you like. It can be used to record dreams, psychic experiences or any odd happenings which you consider are relevant to your progress. It can also be used to keep track of the Lunar phases, astrological aspects and natural cycles of the year. Besides being a useful aide-mémoire the magical diary provides an additional act of self-discipline, giving a sense of routine to your magical work.

Magical alphabets

In addition to the various ritual equipment used by the magician there is also the employment of magical alphabets. These are used for writing spells or inscribing talismans. In the Middle Ages these secret alphabets were utilised to conceal magical knowledge from outsiders but today are a useful concentration aid. In those workings where magical intentions are written down they provide a good focusing medium. The effort of translating English words into one of the magical alphabets and copying them down on to a piece of paper helps the subconscious mind to absorb the information.

In addition to the magical alphabets given here (Figure 6) there are several others which have been widely credited with magical or occult powers. These include the Hebrew alphabets, the Ogham, the Runes, the Druidic or Coelbran and the Enochian alphabets. They have not been included in this book because they have their own occult mysteries which make them unsuitable for use as ordinary magical alphabets. Any reader who is interested in these alphabets can consult the existing literature which describes their magical and occult uses.

Once you are an accomplished magician you should be able to perform your own workings anywhere within reason. The beginner however will find it easier to use ritual accessories and perform workings within a controlled environment. Ritual workings performed in an atmosphere where candles are the only source of light, where perfumed incenses are burnt and the correct symbolic tools are used transcend the theatrical and can be a very powerful experience.

The use of ritual symbolically divorces the acts of the magician from the limitations of the outside world where magic is something that is derided. Ritual places the magician in a psychological state which allows the hidden powers of the mind to be liberated. However, ritual should never be regarded as an end in itself, but as just another magical tool to assist you to achieve the end results of your efforts.

Theban alphabet

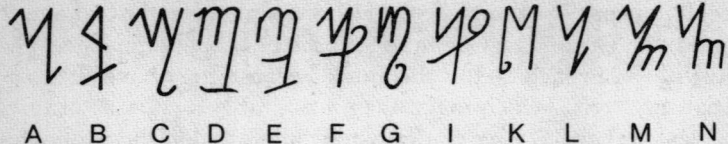

A	B	C	D	E	F	G	I	K	L	M	N		

O	P	Q	R	S	T	V	X	Y	Z	W

Passing the rivers

A	B	C	D	G	H	I	K	L	M		

N	O	P	Q	R	S	T	V	Z

6 The magical alphabets.

46

Malachim script

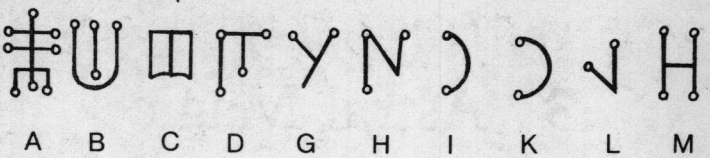

A B C D G H I K L M

N O P Q R S T V Z

Celestial script

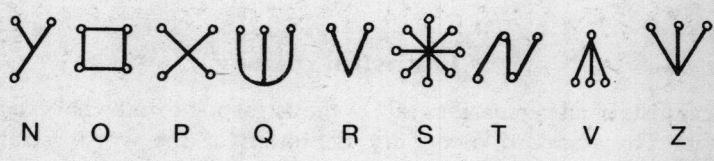

A B C D G H I K L

M N O P R S T V Z

3 Astral Magic

The astral plane

Occultists of all persuasions talk of the astral plane, but what exactly is it? The standard dictionary definition of the word astral is 'connected with or consisting of stars'. In ancient times the astral spirits were the guardians of the stars and appear in classical mythology as the planetary gods or in Biblical lore as the archangels

Whether the astral plane is an actual place or a level of consciousness is a question often posed by those who have only just become interested in occult matters. Many people accept its reality without ever questioning what it represents yet any steps taken on the magical path must be taken with clear knowledge of what is involved.

In the magical context the astral plane is the level of existence where cosmic power manifests into the physical forms we see on the material plane. Some modern scientists have now realized that the universe is multi-dimensional and are on the verge of 'discovering' the astral as the archetypal reality that is the foundation of the physical universe. To the magician the astral plane is the shadow world of the subconscious populated by ancient gods, mythical beasts and immortal heroes. It is the magical realm we enter when we are asleep and the memories of these visits are recalled in a jumbled form the next morning in those vivid dream images we find brightly coloured and often disturbing.

Because the astral plane is composed of plastic mind stuff it can be imprinted with the thoughts of those who investigate its shifting levels. If we think of it in a positive way then the astral regions we explore will be a beautiful place. Conversely, if we have a negative attitude towards it then it can be a frightening place reflecting everything which is dark and unbalanced in our own psyches. To the magician the astral plane represents the world of force while the material plane is the world of form.

It has already been said that we enter the astral plane in our dreams. In general, while confined to the physical body, this is the only contact most people will have with the astral. However, in astral magic you learn how to visit this other reality at will and under control in a conscious state. In the old days this was called 'scrying on the astral' and usually involved the use of a shewstone or crystal. Today modern magicians rely on the power of creative imagination to produce the right conditions for entering the astral plane. Instead of scrying the astral the magician today talks of pathworking techniques.

Pathworking

Pathworking is a magical technique that uses imagination to create dreamlike images while the mind is still in a conscious state. Although these forms of guided meditation are sometimes called fantasy journeying they are more involved than mere romantic escapism. The beginner using the pathworking technique for the first time may simply be an observer of the events he is conjuring up in his imagination but, as he becomes more adept at controlling the pathworking, he will become part of the experience and not just an interested bystander. Events will begin to occur which he has not imagined, plus the realisation that the astral plane is not simply a projection of our mental feelings.

It should therefore be emphasised in our study of astral magic that we are not advocating a retreat into a fantasy world of our own creation in order to escape everyday troubles which, after all, will still be there on one's return from an astral trip. Pathworking should never be attempted without serious intent or without a commitment to learn something of advantage from the experience. Correctly executed, the pathworking technique will cease to be a stereotyped set of imaginative scenes created in your own mind and become a living reality composed of archetypal symbols in which you freely participate.

The key factors in the success of any pathworking are relaxation and the magical triangle of willpower, concentration and visualization. Before attempting any pathworking you must be in a relaxed state. If this is not possible, use the relaxation exercises given in Chapter 1 because only when completely relaxed and free of the tensions of everyday life can the pathworking begin.

Adopt the Egyptian meditation position as described in the relaxation exercise and, as you are symbolically leaving the material world to travel to another level of consciousness, the magical device of a door or gateway will be used to gain entrance to the astral plane. The form this entry takes is, of course, a matter of personal preference. The symbolic entrance could be a glowing triangle through which you pass, the mouth of a cave you enter, a long tunnel with a light at the end or a set of trilithon as seen at ancient stone circles. One of the easiest astral entry symbols to imagine is a door because it relates to the everyday world and we have, therefore, used this symbol in the following simple pathworking exercise.

Read through the text of this pathworking several times before attempting to use it. If possible a second person could read it out while you experience the journey or you could tape-record the text and play it back when you are ready to do the pathworking.

A pathworking exercise

Sitting comfortably in the Egyptian meditation position clear your mind of all outside thoughts and influences. Imagine building up in your mind's eye an oak door of medieval design. See it in full detail. Its surface is rough and covered with knots; run your hands over the door and feel just how rough it is. The door has a handle in the shape of a large iron ring; lift up the handle, note how heavy it is in your hand. Slowly turn the handle. It is stiff from lack of use and you have to assert considerable effort to move it. You push hard against the door and it opens with a loud creaking sound.

Facing you is a thick grey mist. You step forward through the doorway leaving the door open behind you. The mist surrounds you on all sides and it is difficult to see through it. Slowly it begins to clear and you find that you are standing in the middle of a large green field. The Sun is shining and the sky makes a blue dome above you.

In the distance across the field you can see a figure standing but it is too far away for you to identify. The figure beckons you forward and, as you approach, you can see that it is an old man. He is wearing a long, hooded robe like a monk's habit and is leaning on a wooden staff. As you reach him he turns and begins to walk towards a grove of trees on the other side of the field.

You follow the hooded figure and enter the grove. At the centre of the ring of tall trees is a pool of still, clear water. A naked woman kneels by the pool. Her hair falls in long tresses down her back and she holds two pitchers filled with water. As you watch she pours one of these into the pool and the other on to the ground.

The woman gathers some water up from the pool in a pitcher and offers it to you. The old man gestures that you should accept this gift. It is a hot day and you are thirsty so you take the pitcher and drink the cool water.

Suddenly you become aware that the Sun is dipping behind the horizon, The sky is now a deeper blue and the first stars are shining in the dusk. Time changes fast here. The sky is now black and studded with glittering stars which seem more prolific than you have seen them before and brighter than usual. You look down from the sky to the pool but the woman has gone. All you can see is the reflection of your own face shining in the light of the stars.

The old man indicates that it is time for you to leave the grove. He has produced a lantern from his robes and, guided by its light, you follow him across the darkened field. A thick mist begins to gather in front of you and looming through it can be seen the open door through which you entered. You turn to say goodbye to the old man but he has gone. You step through the door and close it behind you. The journey is finished.

Symbolic meanings

As you will have realised, this pathworking has been based on the Tarot card known as The Star. The person who led you across the field to the sacred grove was The Hermit who represents the higher self, guardian angel or spiritual guide. He shines the light on the magical path for the beginner with his lantern. The staff he holds is another form of the magical wand which, as we noted earlier, is a symbol of wisdom, intelligence, communication and the hidden powers of the mind. So, as a participant in the inner journey, the figure represents your higher aspirations to walk on the magical path and become an adept.

The sacred grove of trees has several meanings on an esoteric level. It symbolises the magical circle of wholeness and divine unity. It also represents the earliest temples in which humanity gathered to worship the Old Gods or the archetypal images of the life force. Inside the natural magical circle is a naked woman representing the feminine principle, the Mother of Wisdom, Sophia. She kneels by a pool of water symbolising the collective unconscious of the human race. This is also the pool of individual consciousness — the astral mind stuff which can be activated by the experienced magician into forms on the physical plane. The pitchers of water she is pouring on to the ground and into the pool indicate that she is in control of this reservoir of astral energy.

Astrologically the woman by the pool symbolizes Aquarius the Water Bearer, the zodiacal sign ruled by Uranus, the planet of magicians. The stars which appear so brightly in the sky indicate that your ultimate goal on the magical path is a long way ahead. On another level of symbolism the stars represent the astral or starry plane which our first inner journey has tentatively explored.

To summarise this journey, you have made contact with your inner self (the hooded figure), been shown that the magical path is one of wisdom (the woman by the pool) and that your goal (the starry heavens) is some distance away but can be reached.

Other pathworkings can be constructed using the symbolism of the Major Arcana of the Tarot cards which is a safe route to self-enlightenment. As you progress through this book you will encounter other pathworkings which can be introduced into your workings. At first you may find that you have to concentrate very hard to see the mental images you are creating in your imagination but, after a while, they will appear more easily.

You may also experience spontaneous happenings. Symbols or images you have not created will appear of their own accord. The figures you encounter in your pathworkings may speak to you. Record all these incidents because they will be important.

As you begin to master the art of pathworking you will learn to reach a point in each journey where the imaginative process ends. At these points the flow of images, impressions and symbols will carry on as if they have a will and purpose of their own. Once this has happened you will know that you have established your contacts on the astral plane and been accepted by the powers-that-be.

Reading the Akashic Records

Another form of pathworking is reading the Akashic Records. Akasha is an Eastern word which means the essence of the astral light. Because the astral plane is the level of consciousness preceding physical manifestation many magicians believe that all the knowledge in the universe is available if one can learn to tune in to it.

Obviously such a theory opens up a Pandora's box of possibilities for not everyone is capable of interpreting or understanding the upper limits of knowledge. We can only understand in relation to our own intellectual and spiritual stage of development. This is the fail-safe mechanism built into the cosmic pattern which prevents the misuse of arcane knowledge.

Because the Akashic Records contain all the knowledge of the universe since its beginning they can be consulted to discover details of past incarnations. Again, the extent of the information released from inner sources is in direct relationship to the personal development of the seeker. A morbid curiousity about past lives is unhealthy, as is the desire for self-aggrandisement through knowledge of a past life as a famous or spiritually developed person.

Both these negative attitudes would preclude a seeker from gaining any insight into his previous cycle of incarnation. A legitimate reason for acquiring such knowledge from the inner levels would be if you wanted to work out some karmic problem which was causing your present life to be disrupted. In such case access to the Akashic Records would be allowable.

We will give an example pathworking which can be used to extract information from the Akashic Records. It should be remembered that in the form in which it is given here it is an imaginative journey to the Hall of Records. Unlike the previous pathworking, however, the seeker will be placed in a position where the denizens of the astral plane will communicate directly.

The pathworking begins with the visualization of the door used to symbolise the entrance to the astral plane. Passing through the door you find yourself in the grey mist on the other side. Walking forward through the mist you slowly begin to perceive the landscape around you.

You are standing in a forest. The trees are a mixture of Scandinavian firs and common English trees such as oak, ash and birch. Above the leafy branches the Sun is shining and a warm breeze stirs the leaves. A path, worn bare by countless feet, leads between the trees. At the beginning of the path stands your guide who you recognize from our previous journey. He is an old man in a hooded robe leaning on a staff and beckons for you to follow him along the path.

You have walked some distance now and the forest on either side of the path has become more and more dense. In this part of the wildwood the Sunlight finds it difficult to penetrate the trees and there is a strange, green half-light. Suddenly the path ends. You are standing on the edge of a large clearing in the centre of the forest. Huge primeval trees with enormous trunks and twisted roots rise up on all sides.

In the middle of the clearing you can see a small stone building resembling an ancient chapel. It is made of weathered grey stone and is partly covered with dark green ivy. It has a door very similar to the one you used to enter the astral realm. This door is half open and you push it the rest of the way and enter the building while your guide remains outside leaning on his staff.

Once inside, the building seems much larger than when viewed from outside. The floor below your feet is composed of black and white tiles arranged in a checkerboard pattern. The stone walls seem to be glowing with a soft light, the only illumination in the interior.

Your attention is drawn to a misty figure sitting at the rear of the building. As you walk forward the figure becomes clearer. It is a young woman dressed in blue robes sitting on a high-backed chair. She sits between two pillars and on her lap is an old book with a leather cover fastened by a gold clasp. She smiles and gestures you closer. As you approach she opens the book on her lap. A brilliant white light blazes from between its cover and for a few seconds you are dazzled by its brightness.

Slowly the light fades and you can see that the book has been transformed into a crystal which the woman is holding in her cupped hands. You gaze into the crystal and gradually symbols begin to form in its depths. These symbols flash by as if on a flickering film and are very quickly replaced by pictures of the past, present and future. Some of these pictures flash by too fast for you to see them. Others are seen clearly and will be remembered when you return to the material plane.

The brilliant white light appears again and once more you are looking down at the yellowed pages of the old book. The woman closes the book and refastens the gold clasp. She looks straight at you and her eyes seem to be gazing into your soul. 'Go in peace' she says 'for you have looked into the mysteries of the Book of Life and have been made wise. Return in safety to your earthly abode by the way you entered my realm.'

You bow to the seated figure, turn and walk towards the open door through which you entered the Hall of Records. You pass through and step out into the forest glade. You glance back and the building you have just left has vanished. The guide motions you forward and on to the woodland path leading through the forest.

After some distance walking on the path the way ahead is obscured by the thick grey mist which hangs between the lower branches of the trees. You walk forward into the mist, leaving your guide standing on the path waving goodbye. In front of you is the open door which you step through. The inner journey has come to an end.

A few minutes after the pathworking is finished try to remember the symbols and pictures you saw in the crystal held by the woman in the Hall of Records. Write the details of these down in your magical diary for future reference.

As you progress with the pathworkings you may find that the form of the guide you encounter as you cross through to the astral plane changes. You may find he (or she) takes on the physical appearance of somebody you know, love or trust. Alternatively he may become a mythological figure such as the Arthurian wizard Merlin or the Egyptian god of the dead, Anubis. Whatever form your guide takes, remember that he is the hooded hermit representing your higher self, who you encountered on your first inner journey to the sacred grove.

The magical mirror

Another aspect of astral magic is the use of the magical mirror. This is a traditional device still used for exploring the astral and is a modern version of the ancient shewstone. Just like a crystal or a bowl of water, the magical mirror acts as a reflector of your own inner psychic energies, enabling you to make contact with the astral world.

The construction of a suitable magical mirror is not difficult even for a person who does not have practical skills. The mirror should be made when the Moon is waxing towards Full and can be constructed from a round, concave piece of glass. Using matt black paint, coat one side of the glass (the convex side) with several thick layers so that it is evenly covered. The mirror can then be mounted into a square of hardwood and placed in an ordinary wooden picture frame. A flat mirror can be made in the same way by coating the back of a piece of square glass with black paint and then mounting it in a heavy picture frame.

Once manufactured, the magical mirror should be consecrated in the same way as your magical tools. The blessed water should be applied to the surface of the mirror with a new cloth or sponge and then wiped dry with a separate cloth

The mirror can be used in several ways in astral magic. It can be utilised as an alternative to the imaginary door we visualized as the entrance to the astral plane in the pathworking. To use the mirror for this purpose, place it about two feet in front of you, on a level with your normal field of vision. Burn a candle behind you as the only source of illumination.

Breathe slowly and to a regular rhythm of 1 — 2 in and 3 — 4 — 5 out. Close your eyes and visualize the room in which you are sitting. When you can see every minute detail including the burning candle, the mirror and yourself sitting in front of it, open your eyes again.

Imagine that your body is expanding. It is becoming bigger and bigger and is filling the room.

Now imagine that you are becoming smaller, contracting back to normal size. But do not stop there, keep reducing until you are small enough to pass through the mirror. Look at the mirror and imagine yourself travelling through it and passing out the other side. When returning repeat the exercise, remembering to transform yourself back to normal size once through to the other side.

The second way to use the mirror in astral magic is for pyschic vision. In this exercise sit as before, looking at the mirror, and breath in and out to a regular rhythm. Concentrate your vision on your own face which will be seen dimly in the mirror. Do not stare without blinking as that can cause eye strain. Look beyond the image reflected in the mirror, try to look through the image as if it does not really exist. As soon as you feel any element of tiredness, cease the exercise and try another day.

Eventually you may find that the image in the mirror will be replaced by another face. This may be your spirit guide, a departed relative or someone who is not known to you. Symbols or pictures may materialise, similar to the ones seen in the crystal held by the seated woman in the Hall of Records. A person seen in the mirror may communicate by using thought transference or telepathy; the figure's lips may not move yet his/her voice will be clearly heard in your mind. In some cases the voice may speak in the room so that others who are present may hear it.

When you have finished using the mirror it should be treated exactly like your magical tools. It should be wrapped in a black cloth and put away safely in a special cupboard or drawer. On no account let it be exposed to Sunlight or strong artificial light. The surface of the mirror will respond to the rays of the waxing or full Moon. It can be charged or magnetised by leaving it exposed to direct Moonlight for long periods.

Astral projection

One of the most well-known aspects of astral magic is the use of astral projection to travel on the material plane. The belief that the human body has an astral double which can leave the physical vehicle and travel at will is a very ancient one. The astral double is an exact replica of the physical body except that it is far less dense. Because of this quality (scientists would say that its molecular structure vibrates at a higher rate than the physical) the astral double can pass through solid objects and travel at the speed of light.

Under normal circumstances the astral and the physical bodies remain united. In cases of serious illness, sudden shock, or at the point of death the astral body can project and be liberated from its physical vehicle. There are many cases of ordinary people experiencing astral projection whilst unconscious during an operation, after a car accident or when they have a high fever. They report the experience as floating above the scene, free of their physical bodies, looking down at them as interested but detached observers.

Some religions teach that the astral body is attached to the physical by what is referred to as the silver cord. This is the astral equivalent of the umbilical cord that attaches an embroyo to its mother's womb before birth. On death the silver cord breaks and the astral or spiritual body is released from its physical vehicle of incarnation. This momentous event may occur immediately after death or any time during a three-day period after the physical body ceases to function. It must be stressed that the silver cord is attached to the physical body during astral travel so there is no danger of the link between the two being broken.

Several methods exist to liberate the astral body from its physical host. One of the most common and safest is given below. In carrying out this exercise it is taken for granted that the would-be astral projector possesses a strong desire to leave his body. This strong feeling is very important if the exercise is to be successful.

Exercise to liberate the astral body

The exercise can either be carried out seated in a chair in the Egyptian meditation position, lying on the floor supported by cushions or on a couch or bed. As with all the exercises in this book, the relaxation technique should be performed prior to its commencement if you are feeling tired or tense.

Now that you are completely relaxed, close your eyes and

visualize the room and everything in it. Imagine it in the smallest detail down to the colour and texture of the furnishings and the objects it contains. When you have done this open your eyes and imagine that you are no longer in your body but are standing in front of yourself. This sounds difficult but is quite easy to accomplish in fact. If it helps, imagine yourself sitting or standing in front of a mirror looking at your reflection.

Gradually withdraw your consciousness from your physical body and into your astral double. Visualise yourself standing looking at your seated or prone body and feel that it is not part of you. Your 'new' body feels much lighter than your physical body and you feel capable of going or travelling anywhere you like.

Turn away from your physical body and move towards the wall. You are not walking but floating a few feet above the floor. As you reach the wall it begins to fade and you are able to pass through to the outside. Glide upwards and you will find yourself above the roofs of the houses near your own home. You can see every detail of the houses, even the missing tiles on the roof.

You are now astrally projected and can travel anywhere you wish. Be aware at all times that even though you are experiencing an ecstatic feeling of freedom you are still attached to your physical body by the silver cord.

When you are ready to return to your body you need only clearly state your firm intention to return and your astral and physical will once again be united. When carrying out this form of astral magic for the first few times it is best to have a set goal in mind, such as a visit to a friend or to a particular place. It does not matter if you have previously visited that place or not while in the physical body.

When making astral house calls on others you should observe the normal rules of polite conduct and respect others' privacy just as if you were making a physical visit. Astral spying is morally unforgivable.

Astral magic is one of the most interesting magical techniques. It is also the easiest providing you have a well-developed imagination and the power to visualise clearly and strongly.

What you have learnt about pathworkings on the astral plane, the reading of the Akashic Records, magical mirrors and the techniques of astral travel will be of use as we explore the other forms of magic described in this book.

4 Natural Magic

In our review of the different types of magic practised today we come now to natural magic. As the term suggests, this refers to the magical energies, symbols and accessories which are related to the natural world. In order to understand how natural magic works we first have to examine the beliefs of the ancient peoples who worshipped nature as a manifestation of the divine.

The belief that divine powers could be contacted through nature is the basis of all the early religions. The early humans believed that everything was permeated by the life force. This included inanimate objects like rocks, trees and rivers which were believed to possess a life force personified as either nature spirits or gods. Unfortunately, when the Church replaced the old pagan religions these nature gods were transformed either into demons or the fairies, elves and gnomes of the elemental realm. Such beliefs have been described by anthropologists as animism. The word anima is derived from the Latin meaning 'soul' or 'life'.

In ancient times the Earth was regarded as a deity. Most early civilisations worshipped nature and the Earth in the form of a Great Mother goddess, another title for whom was the Lady of All Wild Things due to her dominion over the natural fauna and flora. Although generally the Earth spirit was personified as a feminine force there was also a male aspect of the life force. He was represented by the ancient gods of vegetation and trees such as the Greek goat foot god Pan, the Roman god of the woods, Sylvanus, the Celtic stag god Cernnunos and the medieval Green Man.

Although the old nature religion was suppressed by the coming of the new faith, many aspects of it survived in the natural or earth magic which developed in the Middle Ages. During that period there was a widespread folk belief in the magical virtues of certain plants, especially for healing, in the use of natural charms such as stones, in the existence of the fairy folk and in various popular rites to ensure good weather or the fertility of the crops. All these different types of natural magic were based on the philosophical belief inherited from the old pagan religions that humanity and nature could co-exist in harmony.

As we have seen in earlier chapters, the foundation of practical magic is the use of natural forces. In the chapters on magical principles and astral magic we have seen that in many cases the magical energy used to produce changes in consciousness originate from within the magician. In natural magic the magician becomes merged with the life force as it manifests through the universe. The results he achieves are therefore dependent upon the reaction between those natural forces and the magician.

This is a subtle difference in approach but one that should be considered. We cannot divorce ourselves from nature because we are part of nature, although some forms of spirituality have ignored this fact. Natural magic brings the magician who, symbolically, stands within the centre of his own magical universe, into direct contact with the forces which are responsible for the cosmic pattern which is the blueprint of reality.

Plant and tree magic

The occult significance of plants and trees is very important in natural magic. The ancient magicians believed that herbs had special occult virtues. According to the belief known as the doctrine of signatures, any herb or plant which resembled a specific part of the human anatomy had the power to cure diseases which inflicted it.

For instance, any plant which was bright red in colour was believed to be able to cure diseases of the blood. Spotted or scaly plants cured skin complaints; perforated herbs healed open wounds; plants exuding juices or resins were good for drying up sores; plants that swelled up or were puffy treated tumours; and those that shed their bark or skin were recommended for cleansing the skin.

In magical lore different plants are associated with the signs of the zodiac and their planetary rulers. A short list is given below for guidance.

THE SUN ruling Leo	Marigolds, thyme, heliotrope, sunflower, cinnamon and any orange or gold coloured flower or plant with a strong smell.
THE MOON ruling Cancer	Night-scented stock, convolvulus, moon wort and any white flowers; those with crescent-shaped leaves or growing near water.
MERCURY ruling Gemini & Virgo	Ferns, broom, aniseed, parsley; plants with yellow flowers and fine leaves.
VENUS ruling Libra & Taurus	Roses, primrose, orchids, violets, lily of the valley and any plants with pink, white or blue flowers or those which are delicately perfumed.
MARS ruling Aries & Scorpio	Brambles, holly, thistles, sage and any red flower with an acrid odour or prickly foliage.
JUPITER ruling Sagittarius & Pisces	Marjoram, borage, pimpernel and any plant with purple leaves and flowers and a potent odour.
SATURN ruling Capricorn & Aquarius	Valerian, hemlock, myrtle and any plant which is grey or brown in colour and has a sharp smell.

These flowers, herbs and plants can be used in magical rituals as an additional symbol when planetary forces are being invoked. If you wish to perform a ritual with a Venusian influence (see Chapter 7) place a bowl or vase of roses on your altar or working surface. In a ritual involving psychic matters a flower sacred to the Moon should be used; for money rituals a herb like borage; for a new house myrtle and so on.

A very unusual but worthwhile natural magic ritual to perform is the creation of a magical garden. Gardening is itself a creative magical act in which the gardener (the magician) creates beauty out of nothing just as the cosmic creator did when the universe was created.

The way to create a magical garden is based on astrological and magical flower lore. For instance, one magician known to me consecrated a willow tree in her garden to the Moon Goddess. She planted a ring of white flowers around the tree and positioned nearby a stone unicorn with its horn pointing towards the willow. In esoteric lore unicorns are sacred to the Moon and have a special significance in the feminine mysteries.

In one corner of the magical garden you can plant a small herb patch containing the plants associated with each of the planets and the zodiacal signs. Each of the trees planted in the garden should be those with magical or sacred symbolism. These will include willow, oak, hawthorn, hazel, ash, birch, elder and yew. The meaning of these magical trees is given below.

WILLOW the tree sacred to the ancient pagan Moon Goddess, possibly because it grows near water. In country districts the willow has gained an unwarranted sinister image. Old folklore says that willows pull up their roots and can walk; they have even been accused of strangling passing travellers with their branches. These fairy tales may date back to pagan times and the ancient rites performed in honour of the Great Goddess.

OAK is traditionally the King of the Trees. It was widely regarded as sacred by the ancient Celts and Nordic peoples who worshipped their gods in oak groves. Mythologically the oak is the tree of the sky or thunder god and is associated with the symbol of the lightning flash representing invoked magical energy.

HAWTHORN is a tree which is also sacred to the Goddess. It featured in the medieval revels of May Day when people danced around the phallic maypole on the village green. It is considered unlucky to bring hawthorn into the house because, as a tree of the Goddess, it should only be used outdoors in rites in her honour.

HAZEL is the tree of wisdom in Celtic mythology. Hazelnuts are reputed to be capable of passing divine wisdom from the gods. It was believed that anyone who ate from the sacred hazel tree knew instantly the secrets of all sciences and arts. It was also believed that you could make yourself invisible by making a special wand from hazel wood. The association of the hazel with wisdom is recollected in the old saying, 'This is it in a nutshell'.

ASH was a tree sacred to the Norse people who regarded it as the cosmic World Tree. It was on this tree that Odin hung for nine days and nights to receive the wisdom of the magical runes. The ash tree was used for healing in olden times and it is said the Druids possessed wands made from this wood.

BIRCH is a symbol of fertility and is another Goddess tree. In folklore birch rods are used to drive out the spirit of the old season at New Year. It used to be common practice to beat the mentally ill with birch twigs to allegedly drive out evil spirits. The sacred mushroom with the red cap and white spots which features in many children's fairy tales grows in birch forests. The mushroom was used by ancient magicians to communicate with the spirit world.

ELDER is traditionally a tree associated with witches. It is an old superstition that if a child is placed in a cradle made of elder wood he or she will be stolen by the fairies and a changeling left in its place. Elder twigs were also placed above barn doors by farmers in the old days to ward off the witches who were supposed to ride on Hallowe'en. All these odd beliefs are connected with the fact that the elder is the tree sacred to the Great Goddess in her aspect as the Old Crone (see Chapter 5).

YEW is the last magical tree to be planted in our special garden. It is the tree of death which is probably why it was planted around country churchyards in such profusion. Yew is another tree sacred to the dark aspect of the Goddess who acts as a guide to her human children when they depart this world into the next.

Creating a magical garden will take a tremendous amount of energy, time and planning but the end result will be worth the effort. You will have a sacred place dedicated to magic which you can use for meditation and ritual, knowing that everything in it has not been planted haphazardly but with a definite occult purpose.

Flowers and trees which you may include in your magical garden also have a secret language which has been used in natural magic and floral oracles. Some of their symbolic meanings are given below:

BAY TREE   Glory
BEECH   Prosperity
BELLADONNA   Silence
BIRCH   Fertility
BLACK POPLAR   Courage
BLUEBELL   Constancy
BROOM   Humility
BUGLOSS   Falsehood
BUTTERCUP   Wealth

CAMOMILE   Energy
CANTERBURY BELL
  Acknowledgement
CEDAR   Strength
CHERVIL   Sincerity
CHERRY TREE   Education
CINQUEFOIL
  Maternal affection
CLEMATIS   Beauty
COLTSFOOT   Justice
CONVOLVULUS   Binding
COWSLIP   Grace
CROCUS   Happiness

DAISY   Innocence
DOCK   Patience
DEADLY NIGHTSHADE   Truth

ELM   Dignity

FENNEL   Fascination
FIR   Time
FORGET-ME-KNOT   Love

GERANIUM
  Unexpected meetings

HAWTHORN   Hope
HAZEL   Wisdom
HELIOTROPE   Devotion
HOLLY   Foresight
HOLLYHOCK   Fecundity
HYACINTH   Playfulness

IRIS   Divine messages
IVY   Fidelity

JASMINE   Joy
JUNIPER   Protection

LARCH   Audacity
LARKSPUR   Fickleness
LILAC   Humility
LILY   Purity

MAGNOLIA   Love of nature
MILKWORT   Isolation
MOTHERWORT   Hidden lore

OAK TREE   Strength
ORANGE BLOSSOM   Purity

PARSLEY   Friendship
PERIWINKLE   Memory
PRIMROSE   Merit

RAGGED ROBIN   Wit
ROSE   Love
DOG ROSE   Pleasure
ROSE (Red and White)   Unity
ROSEMARY   Remembrance

SAGE   Virtue
SPEARMINT   Sentiment
SUNFLOWER   Adoration

THRIFT   Sympathy
THYME   Activity
TRAVELLER'S JOY   Safety
TULIP   Fame

VERVIAN   Enchantment

WAKE ROBIN   Ardour
WATER LILY   Purity of heart
WOODBINE   Fraternal love
WOODSORREL   Tenderness

YEW   Death

As we saw with the magical garden, as well as the use of flowers and herbs in occult rituals, trees have always played an important role in magic and religion. The ancients believed in tree spirits, called dryads in ancient Greece, who could be beneficial to humans who invoked their help. Today we may laugh at this superstitious belief in nature spirits as nonsense. However, recent scientific research has revealed that plants possess a rudimentary form of extrasensory perception and can communicate with both each other and human beings.

In the past occultists have used musical notes to make contact with plant devas or nature spirits. It is only recently that scientists have discovered that plants respond to certain types of music and other audio stimuli. Plants and trees also have a energy force-field which can be recorded by scientific instruments and experienced by sensitive humans. There is no reason why the life force within plants and trees should not interact with the human mind to create the archetypal images we recognize as dryads, fairies, devas and nature spirits of traditional folklore and ancient mythology.

Trees have always been regarded as having healing powers. The following is a simple magical healing ritual which can be performed whenever you feel tired, tense or have an emotional problem which you cannot solve. Select a quiet place in which to perform a ritual where you will not be disturbed.

If possible find an oak tree because, symbolically, it is the King of the Woods. You need not wear a magical robe unless there is no likelihood of you being disturbed. However, your feet should be bare so that firm contact can be made between your body and the earth. Choose a tree which is tall and straight and comparatively free of blemishes.

Firstly, make friends with the tree of your choice. You can do this by talking to it, touching it with your hands and circling it in a deosil direction three times. Lean back against the tree and place your hands with the palms flat against the trunk. You are thereby completing a circuit with yourself and the tree. Imagine the tree's cycle of life from its beginnings as a small acorn in the ground into a sapling and then to the mature tree it is today. Imagine the birds and small animals that nestle in its branches, trunk and root system and for which the tree is home.

Meditate on the tree and imagine that you are merging into it. Sense the tree surrounding you. Feel that its bark is your skin, hard and scaly. Imagine that your arms are its branches reaching out towards the sky. Feel that your body and legs are its trunk, standing tall and straight. Imagine that your feet are extending into roots reaching down into the earth below. Feel that your blood is the sap of the tree flowing through its branches.

Green energy is now flowing from the tree into your body, refreshing and healing you. Look up into the branches above and feel the elemental power pouring through the tree and entering your mind, body and spirit.

Slowly imagine the flow of green energy ebbing so that gradually the link between you and the tree is severed. You and the tree are now individual entities, each a perfect being within its own environment.

Thank the tree for its healing power and bless it. A small libation of mead, cider or beer can be poured over its roots as a symbolic offering to the tree's nature spirit or a silver coin can be buried next to it.

Weather magic

Weather magic can also be practised by the magician who is interested in the hidden side of nature. Magical rituals to bring rain or change the weather have been practised by magicians for centuries. In the old days witches were said to have the magical power to whistle up winds and old people predicted the weather with special rhymes. A famous example is: 'Red sky at night, shepherd's delight. Red sky in the morning, shepherd's warning.' This is a reference to the fact that a red dawn sky often preceded bad weather.

One of the simplest forms of weather magic which anyone can practise is cloud splitting. This can be performed to create rain. Select a smallish cloud, preferably on a calm day, and concentrate on it hard. Visualize the cloud breaking in two or into smaller clouds. If you concentrate and visualize hard enough you may be surprised how easy it is to perform this simple magical act.

Rain can be invoked by a simple rite of sympathetic magic. Sprinkling water on the ground, or over a circle of dancers who are stamping their feet on the earth, while reciting a suitable petition to a storm god like Odin may have the desired result. This piece of magic works on the same principle as washing your car just before a downpour.

One of the most powerful forms of occult ritual associated with weather magic is the use of the elemental power of the storm. It should be said that storm magic must only be performed by an experienced person.

During a period when a thunderstorm is imminent the atmosphere becomes charged with static electricity. This provides a reservoir of raw energy which can be used by the skilled magician to boost his magical workings. It also acts as a conductor for mental energy, allowing thoughts to flow faster and more clearly across the ether.

Ideally, storm magic should be performed out of doors but great caution should be taken so as not to place yourself in any danger from lightning. The use of magical tools made of metal or any other electrically conducive material is obviously not to be recommended for such workings.

As the storm reaches its climax the magician should symbolically merge with the elemental powers of wind, rain and lightning which are surrounding his working place. Imagine in your mind's eye the purpose of your magical ritual. Visualise your thoughts being swept along on the wind. As the lighting flashes and the thunder roars, project your mental images of what you desire to manifest. After each lightning flash imagine the magical energy you are projecting becoming more and more powerful. Work in this way as long as you can while the storm is raging at its height and wind down your efforts in synchronisation with the storm as it subsides.

Whether boosting magical energies during a storm or working to bring rain, it should be remembered that we cannot interfere with Mother Nature with impunity just for a whim. After a long dry spell it is permitted to ask for rain when the crops are suffering from the drought. However, meddling with the weather for personal enjoyment is not to be recommended and will soon backfire on the hapless magician who attempts it.

Stone magic

Stones can also be used in natural magic. As we know, everything in the universe contains the life force in lesser or greater amounts. It is a well-known fact that the Akashic Records (images of past events) can be 'locked into' stones and released by psychic means. This includes natural stones and those shaped by human beings into buildings. Stones are good storage receptacles for past energies because they have been in existence for millions of years.

The use of stones or any other object to discover things about the past is called pyschometry and this is an art which can be cultivated by the aspiring magician. By holding a stone the psychometrist can tune in to its unique vibration and receive audio, visual and emotional impressions through his or her nervous system.

Select your stone for this experiment. Place it on your altar as this links it symbolically with your magical work. Pick up the stone and handle it thoroughly, feeling its shape and texture and examining its surface. Place the stone in the palm of your hand and concentrate on it.

Within a short time you should feel impressions such as heat, vibration or even something resembling a very mild electric shock or tingling. Some psychometrists report the stone throbbing in their hands like a beating heart, signalling contact with the life force. After a little while place the stone against your forehead at the position above your eyes where esoteric tradition tells us the third eye is located. You will then see pictures of what has happened to the stone during its long history.

Candle magic

One of the simplest of magical arts which comes under the heading of natural magic is candle burning. It is simple because it employs little ritual and few ceremonial artifacts. The theatrical props of candle magic can be purchased at any department store and its rituals can be practised in any sitting-room or bedroom.

Most of us have performed our first act of candle magic by the time we are two years old. Blowing out the tiny candles on our first birthday cake and making a wish is pure magic. This childhood custom is based on the three magical principles we have constantly referred to in this book: concentration, visualization and will-power. In simple terms the child who wants his wish to come true has to concentrate (blow out the candles), visualize the end result (make a wish) and hope that it will come true (will-power).

The size and shape of the candles you use is unimportant, although highly decorated, extra large or unusually shaped candles will not be suitable as these may create distractions when the magician wants to concentrate on the important work in hand. Most magicians prefer to use candles of standard uniform size if possible. Those which are sold in different colours for domestic use are ideal.

The candles you use for any form of magical ritual should be virgin, that is unused. Under no circumstances use a candle which has already adorned a dinner table or been used as a bedroom candle or night light. There is a very good occult reason for not using anything but virgin materials in magic. Vibrations picked up by secondhand materials or equipment may disturb your workings and negate their effectiveness.

Some magicians who are artistically inclined prefer to make their own candles for ritual and magical use. This is a very practical exercise because not only does it impregnate the candle with your own personal vibrations but the mere act of making the candle is magically potent. Specialist shops sell candle wax and moulds together with wicks, perfume and other equipment.

The hot wax is heated until liquid and then poured into the mould through which a suitably sized wick has already been threaded. The wax is then left to cool and once this has occurred the mould is removed, leaving a perfectly formed candle. Special oil–soluble dyes and perfumes can be added to the wax before the cooling process is complete to provide suitable colours and scents for a particular magical ritual. Craft shops which sell candlemaking supplies can also provide do-it-yourself books explaining the technicalities of the art to the beginner.

Once you have purchased or made your ritual candle it has to be oiled or 'dressed' before burning. The purpose of dressing the candle is to establish a psychic link between it and the magician through a primal sensory experience. By physically touching the candle during the dressing procedure you are charging it with your own personal vibrations and also concentrating the desire of your magical act into the wax. The candle is becoming an extension of the magician's mental power and life energy.

When you dress a candle for magical use imagine that it is a psychic magnet with a North and South pole. Rub the oil into the candle beginning at the top or North end and work downwards to the half-way point. Always brush in the same direction downwards. This process is then repeated beginning at the bottom or South end and working up to the middle.

The best type of oils to use for dressing candles are natural ones which can be obtained quite easily. Some occult suppliers will provide candle magic oils with exotic names. If the magician does not want to use these he can select suitable oils or perfumes from his own sources. The oil-soluble perfumes sold by craft shops for inclusion in candles can be recommended.

The candles you use can be coloured in accordance with the following magical uses.

WHITE   Represents spirituality and peace.
RED   Symbolises health, energy, strength, courage and sexual potency.
PINK   Love, affection and romance.
YELLOW   Intellectualism, imagination, memory and creative mental energy.
GREEN   Fertility, abundance, good luck and harmony.
BLUE   Inspiration, occult wisdom, protection and devotion.
PURPLE   Material wealth, higher psychic ability, spiritual power and idealism.

SILVER   Clairvoyance, inspiration, astral energies and intuition.
ORANGE   Ambition, career matters and the law.

If you wanted to use candle magic for healing you would select a red candle to burn. To pass an exam burn a yellow candle, to gain esoteric knowledge burn a blue candle or for material gain burn a purple one. It is obviously these colours relate to the signs of the zodiac and the planetary forces (see Chapter 7).

The simplest form of candle magic is to write down the objective of your ritual on a piece of virgin paper. You can use coloured paper which matches the candle. Write your petition on the paper using one of the magical alphabets (Figure 6). As you write down what you want to accomplish through candle magic – a new job, healing for a friend, a change of residence, a new love affair, etc. – visualize your dream coming true. Visualize the circumstances under which you might be offered a new job, imagine your employer telling you that your salary has been increased or conjure up a vision of your perfect love partner.

When you have completed writing out the petition, carefully fold up the paper in a deliberately slow way. Place the end of the folded paper in the candle flame and set light to it. As you do this concentrate once more on what you want from life. For additional potency you can transform your wish into an ideogram as described previously.

When you have completed your ritual, allow the candle you have used to burn away completely. You do not need to stay with the candle once the ritual is completed but make sure it is safe and that red-hot wax will not cause damage or a fire. Never re-use a candle which has been lit in any magical ritual. It should only be used in that ritual and then allowed to burn away or be disposed of afterwards.

If you are conducting a magical ritual which involves two people (e.g. an absent healing ritual for a person some distance away) then the second person can be symbolically represented during the ritual by another candle. All you need to do is find out the subject's birth date and then burn the appropriate coloured candle for that zodiacal sign. These are as follows:

ARIES	21 March – 20 April	Red
TAURUS	21 April – 20 May	Green
GEMINI	21 May – 20 June	Yellow
CANCER	21 June – 20 July	Silver

LEO	21 July – 21 August	Orange
VIRGO	22 August – 22 September	Yellow
LIBRA	23 September – 22 October	Pink
SCORPIO	23 October – 22 November	Red
SAGITTARIUS	23 November – 20 December	Purple
CAPRICORN	21 December – 19 January	Black
AQUARIUS	20 January – 18 February	All Colours
PISCES	19 February – 20 March	Mauve

Colour

The use of colour is very important in candle magic in order to tune in to the right vibration. A different system of colour is used in natural magic for healing purposes. Scientists researching the use of colour to change mental states and human health now recognize that colour healing does work.

The magician who is interested in practising this form of healing should remember that the colours we observe in the spectrum are created by the refraction of the light from the Sun entering the atmosphere. The use of colour rays in healing is therefore a very natural magical act. The meaning of the different colours used for healing is given below.

RED cures blood diseases, anaemia, physical tiredness, coughs and colds. The use of this colour ray involves the blood, arteries, heart and the andrenalin-producing centres of the body.

ORANGE heals inflammation of the kidneys, prevents asthma attacks, disposes of gall-stones, helps menstruation, controls epilepsy and helps relieve mental fatigue. This ray is also recommended to overcome sexual repression, emotional inhibitions and shyness.

YELLOW works on the stomach, indigestion, liver disorders, diabetes, skin diseases and nervous exhaustion. This ray purifies the digestive tract and bodily waste disposal organs, stimulates the nervous system and cleanses the pores of the skin.

GREEN heals ulcers, heart diseases, high blood-pressure, hypertension, cancer, headaches, venereal disease and influenza. This ray is a colour of harmony so has a calming effect on ailments caused by stress.

BLUE is the healing energy which assists sore throats, toothache, all infectious diseases, dysentery, gastro-enteritis, inflamed eyes, insomnia, shock and palpitations. The overall effect of this colour ray is to act as a psychic antiseptic.

INDIGO treats eye, ear and nose problems, lung diseases, pneumonia, bronchitis, infantile diseases, alcoholism and mental illness. This ray is a combination of red and blue and acts as a psychic anaesthetic.

VIOLET heals neurosis, sciatica, cramp, cancerous tumours, bladder weakness and urinary problems in general. This is a colour ray which has a profound effect on the central nervous system.

These are the seven rays of healing but there is an eighth, the WHITE ray which contains the potentialities of all the other colours of the spectrum. It can be used to cure any disease or illness which does not respond to any of the other healing rays. It does this by increasing the potential energy of the selected ray.

Magical healing using the seven rays works in two ways. As with all other forms of healing it can be performed absently, with the patient in a separate place to the healer, or by direct contact with the healer and patient in the same place. In the former technique the magician can project the ray which will act on the patient's ailment by using mental visualization.

The magician visualizes the colour energy leaving the point on his or her forehead, designated the site of the third eye, either in the form of a ray or ball of coloured light. He then imagines the patient sitting and receiving the colour ray which surrounds and enters his body. This absent healing technique has a high chance of success if the receiver is in a relaxed or meditative state and this can be arranged by the magician and the patient selecting a mutually acceptable time of the day for the healing to be sent.

When contact healing is required then either the above procedure is repeated, but with the patient sitting opposite the magician in the same room. Or the healer can use the patient's own life force in a self-healing ritual.

In this latter technique the patient is asked to imagine that the selected colour ray is filling the room and is being absorbed into the air. Once this visualization has been achieved the patient is told to imagine breathing in the colour as he would breath air into his lungs. When breathing in the various colours, the red, orange and yellow rays should be seen rising up from the earth before being breathed in. As the patient breathes in the blue, indigo and violet rays he or she should imagine that they are emanating from the sky above. The green ray can be breathed in at an horizontal level.

Earth energy

Natural magic also involves the use of the Earth energy which occultists, dowsers and psychic researchers believe flows across the countryside in straight lines between natural power centres. These straight lines have been called leys and connect ancient sites such as prehistoric stone circles, burial mounds and old churches which were built on the sites of Earth power centres.

The Earth energy, which is just another manifestation of the life force, can be used by the magician for any purpose. Ancient usage at sacred sites suggests that in the past it was used for increasing the fertility of humans, animals and crops as well as for healing purposes. Some remnants of these ancient magical practices survive in folklore and seasonal customs associated with sacred places.

If you decide to use one of these sacred sites or power centres for magical ritual certain precautions are required. It is recommended that no metal is carried on to the sacred ground because its presence interferes with the flow of Earth energy and can negate any magic performed. Secondly, always acknowledge the guardian of the sacred place and ask its permission before conducting any magical or psychic work.

In some cases the presence of the guardian will be felt or may even be seen in psychic vision. Such entities may resemble a dragon or serpent (both archetypal images of the Earth spirit), an ancient warrior or priest, a White Lady, an old wise man, a deva, a Shining One or perhaps a flowing mass of electrical energy.

Remember that the Earth energy is very powerful so great caution will be needed. Natural magic is a simple art but you are contacting elemental forces which control the universe. The aspiring magician should therefore only attempt those rituals he feels experienced enough to handle with competence.

5   Moon Magic

The Moon has always played a very important role in practical magic, both as a cosmic influence and a mystical symbol. On a symbolic level it represents the powers of intuition, clairvoyance, the hidden side of the mind (the subconscious), the soul, the evolving spirit of the human race, the collective unconscious, the feminine principle par excellence, the ancient primeval past, rebirth, motherhood, change, memory and the ebb and flow of the life force.

In ancient religions the Moon was worshipped as a goddess under many different names including Diana, Selene, Artemis, Ceridwen, Tanith, Hecate, Hathor and Ishtar. She was sometimes regarded as the daughter of the Earth Mother but was frequently recognized as a deity in her own right. The earliest effigies of the Moon Goddess are to be found in prehistoric cave carvings. In these she is depicted pregnant and full-breasted, holding a horn or cornucopia which was the prototype of the cauldron/chalice/Grail.

As an archetypal image the Moon Goddess is represented in triple aspect in relation to the Lunar phases. These three aspects are the Maiden or Enchantress (representing the new and waxing Moon), the Great Mother (the full Moon) and the Old Crone or Hag (the waning Moon). Different forms of the Triple Goddess can be found in ancient mythology all over the world.

In relation to Moon magic the Triple Goddess symbolises new beginnings, birth, initiation and uncontrolled or natural psychic energy (the Maiden); fertility, growth, fulfilment and prophecy (the Great Mother); death, rebirth and ancient wisdom (the Old Crone).

Sometimes the Moon Goddess appears in mythology as the three Fates who spin the destinies of humankind on the cosmic loom. They were the rulers of the powers of life and death and guardians of the natural order of existence.

The seasonal cycle of growth, reproduction and decay was controlled by the Lunar Triple Goddess. Ancient calendars were often based on the phases of the Moon because of its important connection with the passage of time. As the Muse the Lunar goddess could also grant the gifts of inspiration and creativity to writers, artists and poets.

Ancient cultures preserved the subtle balance between male and female, represented by the Sun and the Moon, which they regarded as essential to the well-being of their society. Recognition of the masculine and feminine energies of the life force was an essential belief in pagan times. With the Piscean Age the male, Solar influence grew stronger and stronger and the Lunar energies were either ignored or deliberately suppressed. Cosmic balance degenerated into material disorder as the old Lunar mysteries and Moon magic were relegated to the periphery of human consciousness.

As we have seen in our study of natural magic the concept of humanity as separate from the material world is a false one. Esoteric tradition, magic, ancient religions and occult arts such as astrology and divination have always taught the connection between humankind and the universe.

It is now accepted by modern science that the human organism responds to the natural rhythms of the cosmos. Changes in the electro-magnetic fields of the Earth caused by the movement of the Moon and the cosmic influence of the Sun create perceptible emotional, psychological and physical changes in human beings. These biological changes are reflected on the psychic and spiritual levels where the Moon's hidden influence is more subtle but just as powerful.

It is now widely agreed by scientists that the human nervous system is affected by changes in the electro-magnetic field caused by planetary influences. The influence of the Moon on tides is well known but scientific researchers, confirming ancient belief, now believe that the human body and the plant realm are also susceptible to cosmic forces emanating from the Lunar sphere. The Moon's phases can affect plant growth, hence the old folk belief of planting crops by the Moon. It can also have an influence on the human mind and affects both human and animal sexuality.

Moon magic is basically feminine in nature. It corresponds to the intuitive, hidden side of the mind which is the source of all true magic. Because of this fact Moon magic particularly attracts women, especially as their biological rhythms are in tune with the Moon. Women are powerful natural magicians and it is unfortunate that the advanced Solar ethos of the Piscean Age has elevated men to become the dominant participants in magical technology.

Moon magic can also be utilised by men, especially those in whom the feminine principle has been activated. It should be stressed here that we are not talking about sexual gender confusion or sexual preference but the male who has balanced his natural feminine side with his masculine persona. There are many male magicians who are devoted to the Great Goddess in her many forms nowadays.

All aspects of genuine magic recognize that each one of us, man or woman, contains within our psyches the potential of the opposite sex. Only by reconciling these opposites and balancing the masculine and feminine elements within can a person truly become a magical adept. A male magician will find Moon magic a very good path to follow for it will help liberate his feminine or Lunar self which Jung calls the *anima*.

As we discovered in our earlier examination of magical principles, practical magic is the ability to create changes in consciousness and produce corresponding changes or improvements on the material plane. This is accomplished magically by using the power of the subconscious mind which is ruled by the Moon.

Unless we can harness the occult (hidden) power of the subconscious it will remain dormant and the magician does this by projecting magical energy out into the astral to create effects on the material plane of existence. This act of projection is a Solar or male action (irrespective of the gender of the magician) and therefore true magic unites both the male and female aspects of the psyche in the sacred marriage of mind, body and spirit.

The cosmic tides or phases of the Moon have special significance to the practising magician. The complete passage of the Moon's phases follows a monthly cycle of approximately 29.5 days from New Moon to Full Moon. In prehistoric times the ancients used a 28-day Lunar cycle which was related to both the female biological rhythms and a 13-month Lunar year of 364 days.

In fact the world 'month' is derived from Moon and relates back to the ancient system of recording the passage of time by the phases of the Moon. The irrational fear of the number 13 as a so-called unlucky omen also relates to the pagan worship of the Moon Goddess which was forbidden in patriarchal times.

In magical lore the New Moon is the time for new beginnings, for the creation of new opportunities, the visualization of new projects and the establishment of new friendships, business partnerships and general social relationships. As the New Moon begins its journey towards fullness it is said to be waxing. Any new venture begun at the New Moon will increase in strength and success as the Lunar disc grows in the sky. Magical rituals practised at New Moon will reap results by Full Moon.

During the Lunar phase when the Moon is waxing or increasing in size in the sky (between New and Full Moon) rituals can be performed for attracting positive things to the magician. This is especially true between New Moon and First Quarter about a week later. The things which the magician wishes to attract to himself can be material, such as money or a good job, or abstract things such as good influences or an increase in the positive side of the magician's character.

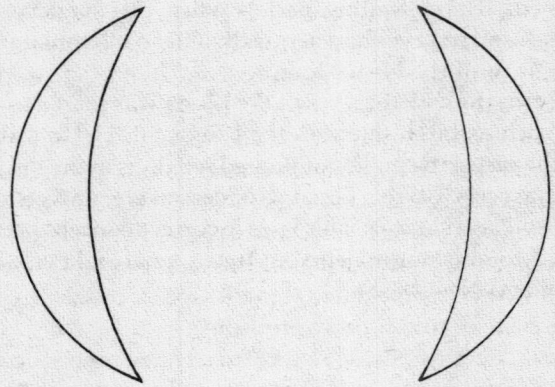

7 Waxing and waning moons.

The period between New and Full Moon is also recommended for astral projection. The three days of the Full Moon especially are regarded as a good time for astral projection because the Lunar energies are at their most potent then. At Full Moon you will find it easier to travel astrally from the physical body. Psychic abilities are also heightened at this time and it is an ideal period for divinatory arts.

After the Full Moon the Lunar energies begin to fade in strength. This period is known as the Waning Moon when the Lunar disc is decreasing in size. Magically this is a time for banishing or rejecting unwanted things and influences from the magician's life or personality.

Negative emotions can be banished during this Lunar cycle; a person can give up smoking or healing rituals can be performed to get rid of diseases or ailments. The treatment of cancerous tumours is recommended on a Waning Moontide. If a house has a unpleasant atmosphere or is haunted by an earthbound spirit the Waning Moontide is a good time to perform a ritual to correct the situation. The best period for performing such rituals is one day after the Full Moon up to the Last Quarter.

The three days before New Moon is the period known as the dark of the Moon. This is a time when the Moon cannot be seen in the sky. Traditionally the dark of the Moon is a period when no magic may be performed. It is a waiting period when the magician takes a natural break and reserves his energies in quiet contemplation before the cosmic birth of the New Moon.

In ancient mythology the dark of the Moon was sacred to the dark goddesses such as Lilith, Hecate, the Morrigan, Hel and the Black Isis. With the rise of the male-dominated religions in the Piscean Age these dark aspects of the Great Goddess were universally con- demned as evil and sinister. This is an incorrect concept because the dark of the Moon is not malefic but forms a natural cycle between the Waning and New Moon.

Lunar pathworking

Contact with the Lunar energies can be made by the practice of the following pathworking or guided meditation. It is recommended that this is performed at the time of the Full Moon, preferably when it is visible in the night sky.

Sit in a chair which gives support to the back in the Egyptian meditation position. Place yourself so that you are able to see the Full Moon clearly. If this is not practicable its rays should be the only illumination in the room.

If you can see the Full Moon look at it for a few minutes remembering to blink naturally. If you cannot see the Moon visualize it hanging in the black sky in its fullest aspect.

Close your eyes and imagine that you are looking at the Moon as if you were an astronaut approaching it from outer space. Gradually the Moon becomes bigger and bigger until it fills your whole vision.

You are now moving across the surface of the Moon. Below you are the crags of the Lunar mountains, the rough edges of the craters filled with inky blackness, the great expanses of open plain covered in greyish brown dust. In the distance you can see the Earth rising above the horizon – a green, white and blue sphere outlined against a black sky studded with brilliant white points of light.

Suddenly, below you in one of the larger craters, you see a flash of silver-coloured light. As if drawn by a magnet, you find yourself dropping down to the source of the light. Upon reaching this you realize that it is a sphere of silver light nearly six feet in diameter, hovering above the dusty floor of the crater.

Unafraid, you move closer and enter the luminous sphere and allow it to encompass you. Turning, you can see the Lunar landscape but it is as if you were viewing it through opaque glass. There is a sensation of movement similar to a high-speed lift and the landscape outside is changed.

You step out of the sphere of silver light on to grass which is glittering with frost. The air is cold and clear and it is night time. In the distance looms a range of jagged, snow-capped mountains which remind you of pictures you have seen of the Himalayas. Although it is night the landscape seems to be illuminated by a soft, silvery light whose source you cannot see.

In front of you a steep path leads down to a deep valley beneath the mountains. As you begin to walk along it you can see a line of figures walking at the bottom of the valley. These people are dressed identically in long white robes. There are men, women and children of all ages, walking slowly in small groups and they are led by a young girl who sits on a unicorn.

She is also wearing a long white robe but has a silver pendant around her neck in the shape of a crescent Moon. She turns to look at you and her eyes shine like the stars you saw above the Lunar landscape. She beckons for you to follow but you resist as her way is not the path you must follow.

Slowly, the line of figures winds its way out of the valley and vanishes into the shadows below the mountains. You begin to walk away from the valley and as you do so a small, black robed figure steps out on to the path from behind a rocky outcrop. The figure has a hood pulled down over its face and it is impossible to tell if it is male or female. Despite its sudden appearance you feel no fear for this is the realm of the Great Goddess and no harm can come to one of her children.

The figure bows in greeting and in a low whispering voice asks what you are seeking in this place. Your reply is that you desire to know the secrets of her realm. The figure nods in reply for your answer has been the right one and gestures with a flowing sleeve for you to follow it along the path. The dwarf-like figure moves ahead, seeming to glide above the ground without touching it.

In the distance, standing in the middle of a snow-covered plain, you can see a crystal dome shining in the strange silvery glow which illuminates this Lunar world. The figure beckons you on and you pass through the outer wall of the dome which feels like walking through a spider's web.

Inside, the crystal dome is lit by a soft white light. Your elfin guide bows towards the centre of the dome. As your eye follows the movement you become aware that three presences sit on silver thrones in the centre of the dome and can feel yourself being overwhelmed by the energy emanating from these three figures.

The first presence you recognize as the young woman who was riding the unicorn across the valley in the company of the white-robed figures. She acknowledges that she recognizes you with a slight nod of the head and a faint smile.

Next to her sits an older woman who could be her mother for she has the same shining eyes but her face is older and wiser. All the wisdom of the world is in her eyes. Her body, partly concealed by a long white robe, is fuller than the young woman's and there is a hint that she may be pregnant. She looks across at the younger woman and they exchange knowing glances.

The third presence in the crystal dome is smaller than the other two women and older. She is bent double with age and wears a silver cloak which shadows her face except for her eyes which burn bright with the energy of youth.

In front of the three women stands a huge silver cauldron supported on three legs. The rim of this magical vessel is studded with huge, milky white stones which seem to glow with coloured lights. The old woman beckons you forward and you gaze into the cauldron to find yourself looking down into a whirlpool of silver light. Everything begins to spin round and the three presences blend into one and then fade away.

You are standing within the sphere of silver light on the floor of the crater. You step out of the sphere on to the dusty surface of the Moon. The floor of the crater begins to fall away from you and you are looking down at the Moon beneath you. Black sky surrounds you and the Moon is getting smaller and smaller in the distance. Suddenly, you are looking up at the Full Moon in the sky from the Earth. Your journey is at an end.

The above pathworking has been designed to introduce you to the subtle energies of the Lunar mysteries. It uses certain key symbols and images to allow you to tune into the influence of the Triple Goddess.

Moon ritual

The following ritual can also be performed for a similar purpose. Ideally it should be performed out of doors but if this is not possible choose a place indoors where you can either see the Full Moon or its rays.

First, cast your circle in your chosen working place. Before performing the ritual take a bath, remembering that the water is cleansing the spirit as well as the body. For this ritual you will need six candles (blue, white or silver), some incense, a compass and a chalice of natural fruit juice or wine.

Light the incense on the altar and have a representation of the Moon Goddess present where you can see it. Place the chalice on the

85

altar with a lighted candle on each side of it. Sit quietly for a few minutes before commencing this Full Moon ritual.

When you are ready to proceed say aloud the following words:

O Lady of the Moon
Mistress of silver magic
I erect this circle
a sacred place dedicated
to thy name.

Place a lighted candle at the North quarter and say:

O Lady of the Moon
the Earth reaches out for you
it is rich and fertile
through thy power.

Light a candle at the East quarter and say the following words:

O Lady of the Moon
May the air be filled
with thy presence
may the wind sing
thy name softly.

Light a candle at the South quarter of the circle and say aloud the following words:

O Lady of the Moon
thy presence rules
the seasons
may each one bring
forth the glories of
the natural world.

Place a lighted candle at the West quarter and say aloud:

O Lady of the Moon
you are the ruler of the seas

and the tides.
May the oceans flow
clear and pure.

Stand before the altar or in the centre of your circle and raise your arms towards the Full Moon. Say the following words.

O Lady of the Moon
this sacred circle
has been erected
this night to bless
your name.
I do ask that you
grace this circle with
your presence tonight.

Stand for a few moments with arms upraised towards the Full Moon and gaze in meditation at the representation of the Moon Goddess on the altar.

Kneel before the altar and take up the chalice. Raise it three times to the Full Moon and say aloud the following words:

O Lady of the Moon
I pour this libation
in honour of you.

Sprinkle a few drops of wine before the altar and say:

O Lady of the Moon
I drink this toast
in your honour.

Drain the chalice and return it to the altar.

Then sit and relax thinking of the Moon Goddess in her three aspects of Maiden, Great Mother and Old Crone. Meditate on the different forms of magic associated with the Moon Goddess.

At the conclusion of the ritual extinguish the candles around the circle and say the following words:

O Lady of the Moon
thank you for strengthening
me with thy presence.
Mistress of magic
may your love, power and wisdom
be mine.

Perform the banishing ritual of the circle, as previously described, and extinguish the two remaining candles on the altar. Say aloud in a clear voice and with authority:

The rite is ended.

The practice of the Lunar pathworking and the above ritual should ensure that you will contact the Moon energies which will help you perform successful Lunar Magic.

How do you work simple Moon Magic? If you wish to attract beneficial influences towards you then follow the procedure below on either the night of the New Moon or any night of the Waxing Moon, especially up to First Quarter. Information on the phases of the Moon can be found in most good diaries or in the astrological pages of PREDICTION.

Take a piece of plain virgin paper. Draw on it the symbol of the Waxing Moon (Figure 7). Underneath write what you wish to achieve using one of the magical alphabets. You may want a better job, improved health or perhaps an increase in salary.

Take your time writing out the petition. Be specific and always write it in ink not pencil which can be erased easily. Do it as carefully as you can, making sure that each character is drawn correctly. While you are writing out the petition, visualize the events that you want to happen coming to pass.

When you have completed the petition, carefully fold up the paper. Keep it on your person at all times until the night of the Full Moon when it should be destroyed completely. During the period from New to Full Moon your petition should have been answered.

If you want to banish unwanted influences from your life – such as poverty, illness and bad luck – then any night from the second day after the Full Moon until three days before New Moon (and especially from Full Moon to Last Quarter) take a piece of plain white paper. Draw on this the symbol which represents the Waning Moon (Figure 7) and underneath write, in the magical script of your choice, your petition to banish the unwanted influences. This banishing petition should be destroyed before the New Moon.

If you want to attract several different things on the nights of the New or Waxing Moon or banish on the nights of the Waning Moon then you must write out a different petition for each of them. Do not forget to destroy the petitions completely before the allotted expiry date otherwise the magical force will be negated.

The use of the Full Moon for divination has been mentioned previously. A simple ritual for this purpose is given below.

For this you will need six white, blue or silver candles, a compass and some incense. In addition you will also need a divinatory tool such as the Tarot, crystal, runes, etc. As this is a ritual dedicated to the Moon Goddess, a traditional form of Lunar divination, a bowl of water, has been used. Preferably this should be spring water but, if you cannot locate a well or spring locally then bottled spring water from your local health food store or supermarket is permitted. Place the half-filled bowl of water on the altar, together with some white flowers which are sacred to the Moon Goddess.

Perform the circle opening and light two candles on the altar and four around the cardinal points. Light the incense and say the following words:

> O Lady of the Moon
> Mistress of the silver magic,
> Guardian of the gates of
> astral plane,
> I cast this circle on the
> night of the Waxing/Full Moon
> in thy honour.

Take the incense from the altar and walk three times around the circle deosil (clockwise). Return the incense to the altar and say aloud the following words:

> O Lady of the Moon
> open up the gates of the
> Otherworld

that future events
may be discerned.
Make my inner eye
clear and strong
that it may penetrate
the veil between this world
and the next.
Let that which is to come
to pass be revealed.
The Moon is high in the sky
and those with eyes to see
may gaze beyond to the mysteries
hidden behind its face.

Meditate on the purpose of your divination. Take the bowl of water in both hands and gaze into it. Do so without staring too hard and blink normally. Be relaxed. You may not get instant results but with perseverance you will begin to see shadowy shapes, coloured lights and eventually symbols and images which will have meaning to you.

When you have completed your divination return the bowl of water to the altar. To end the ritual say aloud the following closing words:

O Lady of the Moon
Mistress of silver magic,
Guardian of the astral plane
I thank you for your help
this night of the Waxing/Full Moon
in revealing the shape of things
to come.

Banish the circle in the normal way and extinguish the candles and incense safely.

Moon magic is one of the most rewarding forms of magical technique. It is also one of the most important. Magicians believe that the feminine Lunar energy is the aspect of the life force which is used to produce magical effects on the astral. When these are transferred into physical happenings on the material plane that is true magic.

6   Elemental Magic

In ancient times occult philosophers divided nature spirits into four separate classes. These divisions corresponded to the four natural elements of Fire, Earth, Air and Water. The different spirits or personifications of the elemental forces were named by Paracelsus in the following way. The spirits of Fire are called salamanders, the spirits of the Earth are called gnomes, the spirits of the Air are called sylphs and the spirits of Water are known as undines.

It is believed that Paracelsus derived these names from the Greek *salambe* or fireplace, the Greek *gnoma* meaning knowledge, the Greek *silpha* meaning butterfly and the Latin *unda* which means a wave. In accordance with their elemental qualities the salamanders appear to psychic vision in the shape of creatures made of living flame. The gnomes are small, dwarfish figures, brownish grey in colour. The sylphs are wispy, airy creatures and the undines are of a watery composition, coloured green or blue.

The elemental guardians

Occult lore assigns each of the elemental realms with a guardian. These are known as Djinn, ruling the Salamanders; Ghob, ruling the gnomes; Paralda, ruling the sylphs; and Niksa, ruling the undines. These elemental guardians are represented in the Tarot as the Kings and Queens of the Swords, Pentacles, Batons, and Coins for they can appear as either sex.

Djinn appears to psychic vision as a fire giant. His lithe body is composed of twisting flames and his slanted eyes glow red. Ghob appears as a squat, heavy creature, dense in form. He usually manifests in the traditional fairy-tale gnome or goblin figure and exudes an aura of old age, strength and wisdom. Paralda is a writhing figure, composed of pale blue or grey mist. His form is tenuous and indefinite, always changing shape. Niksa also appears fluid. His greenish-blue aura flows back and forth, splashed with silver streaks and grey tentacles of power.

The descriptions of these elemental guardians are the magical or telesmatic images used by magicians to contact the relevant force. It is true to say that these are imaginative images of each of the elemental guardians. However, it is how they will appear to the psychic vision of the person who evokes them and how they should be visualized by the magician working elemental magic.

The practice of elemental magic is concerned with the invocation of the elemental forces of the universe which are represented by the elemental spirits and their four guardian rulers. While modern scientific discoveries have revealed many different forces at work creating and sustaining the universe, the magical cosmos was composed of the quadruplicate foundation blocks of Fire, Earth, Air and Water.

These elemental forces are represented in the ancient book of wisdom known as the Tarot, symbolised by the four working tools of the practising magician and the sub-divisions of the zodiacal signs in astrology. They should not be regarded merely as physical energies for they are also spiritual in nature. In esoteric teachings the oneness of spirit and matter is emphasised.

Because the Hermetic axiom teaches 'As above — so below' the elemental forces are reflected both in nature and in the human psyche. The significance of the four elemental forces is given below while their correspondences in magical working will be found in the appendix.

The elemental principles

WATER is described as the elemental principle of movement and change. As water changes constantly it represents the changing moods of our emotional self, including romantic love. The element of Water therefore has rulership over our imaginative faculties, inspiration, extrasensory perception, dreams, feelings, purification, emotions, fertility, friendship, pleasure and love. The colour assigned to this element is blue and it is regarded as feminine in nature.

Our bodies are made up of 90% water and it is from the waters of the womb that we make our first entry into the physical world. In many ancient myths the sea, symbolic of the womb of the Great Mother Goddess, is regarded as the birthplace of all life. This ancient belief is confirmed by modern science.

EARTH is the elemental principle of endurance and stability. It is the physical plane on which we incarnate to progress through the school of experience known as life. The natural world around us is not to be ignored as a dangerous illusion but accepted as the environment in which spiritual lessons are taught. The Earth element has rulership over material matters, growth, death, abundance and fertility. The colour of Earth is either green or brown and it is generally regarded as having a feminine influence.

In the pagan old religions the Earth was regarded as the Great Mother Goddess. This belief survives today in the popular term Mother Nature and the description of pregnant countrywomen as 'Earth Mothers'. Recently scientists have speculated that the planet Earth is a living organism and, interestingly, have called this entity Gaia after the Greek earth goddess.

AIR is the elemental principle of adaptibility and expansion. It rules the intellect, that tool which we use to make sense of the universe by projecting our philosophical ideas on to it. On a magical level the element Air has rulership over intelligence, visualization, communication, memory, intellectual knowledge and mental concentration. The colour of Air is yellow and it is regarded as masculine.

In most ancient religions Air has been associated with the free-flowing energy of Spirit. Wind and breath has always universally been regarded as a symbol of the life force. In the Tarot, which although it is of early medieval origin preserves ancient esoteric knowledge, the spiritual element of Air is represented by the Major Arcana card *The Fool*. Beneath the motley jester's costume he is the magical adept travelling the endless path through life, experiencing through his intellectual senses.

FIRE is the elemental principle of energy and force. It has rulership over healing, physical energy, creativity, destruction, purification and sexuality. In the magical context Fire represents the will-power of the magician which must be channelled to produce the desired effects. If the will becomes perverted or out of control then the end results will be very disruptive to both the magician and those around him. Fire is a very potent elemental force and must be controlled to gain the maximum benefit. The practice of magic is not for the weak in spirit and contact with the Fire element will soon separate the proverbial sheep from the goats. The elemental colour of Fire is red and it is masculine in nature.

In ancient myths fire was the gift of the gods to humanity and since its discovery it has been regarded as a sacred force. On special festival days sacred fires were lit on hillsides. These fires were symbolic of the energy and light of the Sun. Fire was also widely regarded as a symbol for spiritual illumination.

Because each of the elemental forces can be found in our human psychological make-up they can be used to correct imbalances in the psyche. Some examples of the way in which the elemental qualities can appear in either positive or negative form in the human psyche are given below.

The elemental qualities

WATER   The positive influence of this element manifests as a person who is emotionally balanced and with a constructive imagination. Such a person may experience powerful dreams or psychic visions. Positive Water types will be sensual, romantic and creative, with a good understanding of others' emotions and feelings. They are good listeners who put people at ease and are regarded as sympathetic.

When the Water element is operating as a negative influence in the psyche then the afflicted person will be emotionally unstable, vague, indecisive, wishy-washy, devious and dreamy. Such a person is usually described as 'wet' or a 'drip' in accordance with his/her negative elemental qualities. He may suffer from depressions, bad moods, indifference to others and be self-centred to the point of suffering from delusions or hypochondria.

EARTH A person who is positive Earth will have a personality that is practical, methodical and constructively critical. His actions will express stability and his general outlook will be reliable and realistic. Such people will probably be very good with their hands, be expert craftspeople and possess the virtue of unlimited patience in any irritating situation.

If the Earth element is unbalanced in the personality this will be expressed as boredom, laziness and a lack of enterprise. This type of person will be quite happy to drift through life without direction. Often dull, lazy and impractical, he will suffer from a tendency to be ultra-critical in a destructive way. The intellectual outlook will be rigid and dogmatic.

AIR When this element is positively balanced the personality will have an inquiring mind, a good memory and will be efficient and extrovert in outlook. These people find it easy to adapt to new circumstances, have an inborn ability to communicate with other people and are expert at 'thinking on their feet.'

In contrast, when the Air element is unbalanced the unfortunate person will suffer from a lack of attention to detail and have a tendency towards superficiality. This type of person is hopelessly impractical, is unable to face up to life, finds it difficult to express his or her ideas and will find it difficult to settle down. Such subjects are described as 'having their heads in the clouds' or being 'airy fairy'.

FIRE This element when positively aspected in the psyche creates an individual who is self-assured and energetic. These individuals find it easy to express themselves on all levels, are extroverted, gregarious and have strong control over their emotional selves.

But when this element is expressed negatively it manifests as a person who is individualistic to the point of selfishness and is dictatorial, egocentric and hyperactive. Such people have the potential for extreme violence and are generally aggressive.

Ideally, all the elemental qualities should be balanced in the psyche of a true magical adept but such perfection eludes most of us. However, if you feel that your own elemental forces are imbalanced there is a magical technique which can be used to remedy the situation. This technique uses the four elemental symbols which are sometimes called the Tattwas. These are symbols used in Eastern magical practices which have been adapted to the Western magical tradition.

Elemental colours

For the purpose of this book the traditional colours of the elemental forces used in Western magic have been assigned to the Tattwas in preference to the usual Eastern colour system used in most magical guide books for these symbols. The Tattwas are a silver or blue crescent for the elemental force of Water, a black or brown square for Earth, a yellow circle for Air and a red triangle for Fire (see Figure 8). In this form these symbols can be used to represent the four elemental powers for meditative purposes.

First, copy these symbols on to separate pieces of white card using either paint or a felt pen in the appropriate colour. Select which ever elemental symbol you think represents the quality which is unbalanced in your personality, e.g. the yellow circle of Air if you have a bad memory or find it difficult to talk to people. Place the card at eye level and sit in a chair so that you can view it easily and adopt the Egyptian meditation position.

Look at the card for a few minutes. Imagine that you are leaving your body and travelling towards the elemental symbol. Close your eyes and visualise this happening if it helps to do it that way.

You are now inside the symbol and completely surrounded by it because it is three-dimensional in shape. As it encompasses you imagine that the negative aspects of your personality relating to the element of your choice are being replaced by the positive aspects you desire. If you are using the yellow circle of Air imagine that your memory is improving. Breathe slowly and imagine yourself in a room full of strangers, moving from group to group, joining in with the conversation. When you return from your inner journey you will find it easier to talk to others,

Gradually withdraw your projected consciousness from the elemental symbol. You are now sitting back in your chair and what you have worked for will come about. Do not expect instant results but use this magical technique over a period of time and you should

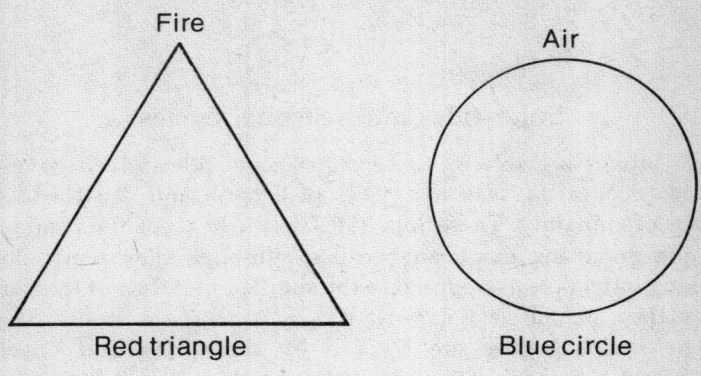

Fire

Red triangle

Air

Blue circle

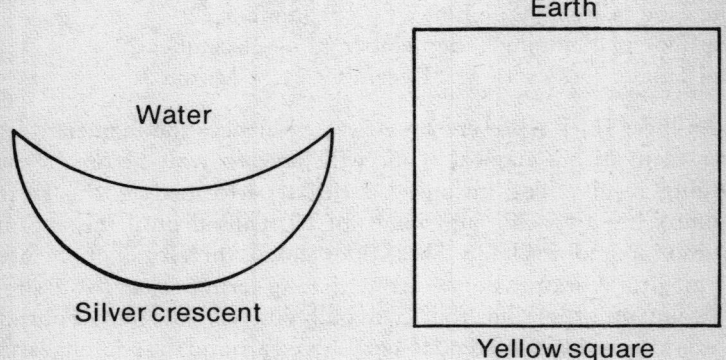

Water

Silver crescent

Earth

Yellow square

8 The elemental symbols of the Tattwas.

be able to notice some changes in the negative side of your personality.

Solar tides and seasonal cycles

The Tattwas are related to certain cosmic tides which have an influence over the seasonal cycles of growth and decay and the affairs of humanity. These Solar tides should be recognised and used by the practising magician because, although they mark slow-moving influences as opposed to the short-term effects of the Lunar tides, they are still very important.

The seasonal tides are marked by the spring and autumn equinoxes, when day and night are of equal length, and the winter and summer solstices, the shortest and longest days respectively. The equinoxes fall on March 21 and September 23 while the solstices are usually on December 21 and June 21. The seasonal periods ruled by the elemental tides are as follows.

The Tide of Sowing: March 21 — June 20
The Tide of Reaping: June 21 — September 22
The Tide of Planning: September 23 — December 20
The Tide of Destruction: December 21 — March 20

As these tides represent long-term influences the magician who uses them in his magical work will have to wait before he sees definite results. For instance, a ritual performed at the spring equinox for a specific aim may not be realised until the autumn equinox six months later. These tides should therefore only be used for magical workings connected with long-term projects or desires.

As you progress along the occult path you will note that important matters in your life will tend to be resolved around the equinoxes and solstices. This is when important changes take place on inner levels. The spring equinox especially can be a time of great upheaval. Friends may suddenly drop out of your life and you may not pick these contacts up again until the autumn equinox, if at all. However, this will be compensated for by new friendships which will begin at or shortly after the equinox.

The dark winter from December to March is the period of ridding yourself of unwanted influences or deciding in which direction you want your life to go during the coming year. This magical action is preserved in the popular custom of making New Year resolutions even if few survive until the end of January.

From the spring equinox to mid-June is the time of new beginnings when fresh plans can be made and ventures begun. From the summer solstice to the autumn equinox in late September you will reap the rewards of past efforts. From the equinox to the midwinter solstice is the time to plan for the future and consider past lessons and mistakes.

These seasonal tides also correspond to a lesser degree to the subdivisions of the magical circle known as the quarters or compass points. Their influences are as follows;

Water   West and dusk
Earth   North and midnight
Air   East and dawn
Fire   South and noon

If you have want to balance the elemental forces, when you have erected your circle in your temple or magical working place visualise images at each quarter to represent the four energies and the time of day associated with their influence. Examples of magical images which can be used for this purpose are given below.

West   A flowing river on a rain-soaked day at dusk
North   A standing stone on a snow-covered moor at night
East   A mountain peak rising from the mist at dawn
Fire   A fire blazing on a square shaped stone.

Pathworking to contact the elements

A more complex method of contacting the four elemental forces is given in the following pathworking. It represents an inner journey during which the seeker encounters symbols of the elemental energies and experiences their influence.

Adopt the Egyptian meditation position. When you are

comfortably seated visualize a door in front of you. It is an old oak door of medieval design. Its handle is a heavy iron ring. Take hold of the handle and turn it. Push the door open and step through.

Facing you is a thick, grey mist. Walk into the mist and feel it swirling around you. It is cold and damp but you hardly notice this. The mist is beginning to clear and you become aware of your surroundings.

You are standing on the side of a steep hill. The hillside slopes away below and there are patches of snow on the ground around you. You are looking down on a wooded valley far below. On the other side of the valley you can see hills similar to the one on which you are standing. Looking up you see a blue sky with scudding white clouds. A strong wind tugs at your clothes and blows through your hair. The wind is cold on your face but the feeling is exhilarating. Your mind seems to be clearer, the cobwebs are being blown away and everything seems bright.

Slowly you begin to walk down the hillside, following a rough path between huge granite rocks. As you reach the lower slopes you find small shrubs growing and wild flowers cling to the moss-covered rocks.

In front of you is a line of trees. As you approach nearer you can see they are fir trees. You walk into the trees and keep walking downwards into the valley below. Gradually the fir trees give way to broad-leafed trees which you recognize as oaks, ash, birch and rowan. You are now entering the wooded valley and keep following the path, drawn by the sound of running water in the distance.

The sun is warm through the branches of the trees. A cool breeze whispers through the canopy of green leaves above you. Birdsong fills the wood and small animals scamper in the undergrowth on either side of the path.

Suddenly the path broadens out into a glade of trees. Sitting in the centre of the clearing, perched crosslegged on a square-shaped stone, is a young man dressed in tattered green clothes of medieval style. He is playing a flute and has antlers branching up from his forehead. As you enter the glade he pauses and looks up at you. As you walk closer to him you can see he has slanting eyes and pointed ears.

The horned man smiles and lifts his left hand in greeting. Despite his bizarre appearance you are not afraid of him. In fact he exudes an aura of calm and protectiveness. You recognize him as the Lord of the Greenwood and it is his domain that you are walking through.

A movement in the undergrowth catches your eye and you look away for a few seconds. When you look back the horned man has vanished. You walk on towards the source of the sound of running water.

A few yards on the path turns to run alongside a swiftly flowing river. It tumbles over rounded grey stones polished smooth by centuries of water flowing over them. You are feeling hot after your long walk through the wood and kneel by the river to splash cool water over your face. As you do so, imagine that the healing energies of the water are washing away all the spiritual impurities and cleansing your inner being.

Refreshed by the cooling water you continue to walk along the riverside path leading up the valley. The river is becoming narrower now and you realise that you must be close to its source. In front of you is a spring bubbling up from a cleft in a group of ancient rocks.

The spring is shadowed by a clump of hawthorn trees. On one of the rocks above the spring a mystical symbol is carved. It is a spiral, representing eternity and the passage of the soul from the infinite back to infinity. This sacred spring is where the river is born, rising out of the depths of the Great Mother Earth to flow along the valley between the hills and out into the ocean below.

Once past the spring the rough grass path you have been following through the woods begins to rise. You are now climbing upward between huge boulders entwined with tree roots. In front of you, between a natural gateway of huge rocks, is a dark entrance to a hillside cave. On either side of the cave mouth is a standing stone carved with the spiral symbol you saw at the spring.

You feel drawn towards the cave as if something inside it is calling you in. Walking forward you pass between the two standing stones and into the darkness. Gradually, your eyes become used to the gloom and you realize that the rock walls of the cave are covered with fungi which glow with a soft light.

Although the cave seemed cold and damp after being outside, it grows warmer as you walk down the passageway from the cave mouth. On the walls are ancient paintings glowing with colour. These depict hunting scenes, stag-headed gods, dancing figures, spirals and goddesses with blank faces. On the floor of the cave are littered numerous animal bones,

The passageway opens out in front of you into a large underground cavern. The walls of this cavern are translucent and behind them vague shadows move, pulsating with a reddish glow. It is as if the underground cavern is alive.

In front of you is a large opening in the floor of the cavern. Looking down into it you can see molten lava and flames. A wave of intensely hot air streams up from the opening, forcing you back to escape the heat.

Lying on the floor in front of you is a rough crystal. It looks as if it has just been hewn from the solid rock surrounding you. The crystal is crudely shaped and is a yellowish grey in colour. Fascinated, you pick up this strange object. It is icy cold to the touch despite the torrid atmosphere in the underground cavern.

As you look at the crystal it begins to clear. Coloured lights are moving inside the crystal and you can see shadows like those behind the walls of the cavern. The crystal is beginning to pulsate in your hand. It is as if you are holding a human heart. The crystal is now glowing with a brilliant white light. The light fills the cavern. All you are aware of is the brilliant white light filling your mind.

It is dark. You are floating in inky blackness. There is no sound. All around you is black nothingness. Silence encloses you completely.

Gradually you become aware of faint pinpricks of light in the darkness around you. These seem to be moving towards you, becoming brighter and brighter. You can now see that they are stars. You are floating in outer space. In the distance you can see galaxies. Spirals of stars circling around an invisible centre, moving like cosmic ships through the vast ocean of space. You are at peace in complete harmony with the universe and the whole of creation.

The stars are fading now. Once more you are surrounded by darkness. Through the blackness you can see a bright light moving towards you. As it nears, you become aware that it is a huge crystal like the one which you picked up from the cavern floor.

You are falling into the crystal. It surrounds you. You are the crystal. Brilliant white light fills your mind. You are standing back in the underground cavern with the small crystal in your hand. It has faded to its original yellowish grey colour.

Replacing the crystal on the floor where you found it you retrace your steps out of the cave. Passing between the two standing stones at the cave entrance you walk down the hilly path towards the spring.

You reach the spring which is the birthplace of the mighty river. Walking past it you continue along the riverbank, following the path. You pass through the wooded glade where you saw the horned man. The air is colder now as you leave the wood and enter the fir tree forest for you are beginning to climb up the hillside. The Sun is setting behind the hills and it is getting dark.

In front of you a thick grey mist is rising from the damp ground. You walk into the mist and it surrounds you. Through the mist you can see the oak door, open as you left it. You walk through the door to the other side and close it firmly behind you.

The inner journey is over now and you should open your eyes.

This pathworking introduces the traveller to the four elemental forces of Air, Water, Earth and Fire. The final encounter in the underground cavern with the crystal leads to an experience of Spirit which is the reality behind the four elemental powers of the natural world.

At the beginning of this chapter the guardians of the four elements were described. They are symbolic representations of the elemental forces in an easily accessible form. If you are practising elemental magic then the evocation of the appropriate elemental guardian is recommended.

If you decide to perform a ritual for material abundance, for instance, then you would call upon Ghob, the Lord of the Gnomes. Imagine him as described earlier in this chapter. Use your pentacle for this type of magic and introduce into your ritual the symbolism of the Tarot's Minor Arcana cards, the Coins or Pentacles, especially the Ace of Coins and the Ten of Coins which both signify material success and gain.

These cards are placed on your altar or working area and used as concentration or meditation symbols. The other Tarot suits correspond to the other three elemental forces. These are Batons (Air or Fire), Cups (Water) and Swords (Fire or Air) and can be used where appropriate in elemental magic rituals, along with the corresponding magical tool as described in Chapter 2.

7 Planetary Magic

In previous chapters the importance of astrological aspects in practical magic has been discussed. This final chapter deals specifically with planetary magic and introduces the use of astrology as an essential working tool for the aspiring magician.

Ancient magicians and priests personified the archetypal forces of the seven classical planets as gods and goddesses. In Babylonia and Chaldea, the region of the Middle East regarded as the homeland of both magic and astrology, the worship of the planetary gods was an important part of religious life. Jewish mystics and magicians were heavily influenced by contact with the Babylonians and the Chaldeans so adopted many aspects of their stellar religion. As a result, the pantheon of planetary gods was assimiliated into Judaism and formed the foundation of medieval magic.

In medieval magic the planetary forces were represented as archangels each of which was given rulership over one of the known planets and the Sun and the Moon. Our system of magical correspondences is largely based on the worship of the Middle Eastern planetary gods who were accepted into Judaism as angels. The archangels appear frequently in Biblical lore as messengers between Jehovah and the Israelites

Behind the bright messengers of light hover the more shadowy figures known to esoteric tradition as the fallen angels. Some Biblical scholars identify these angels with the Ben Elohim or Sons of the Gods who came down to Earth to mate with the daughters of humankind. In Genesis 6:2-7 we read that the offspring of this illicit mating were giants who were the first magicians.

Because of their alleged wicked activities Jehovah sent the Flood to destroy humanity, saving only Noah, his family and an ark of animals. As the legend of the Flood is of Babylonian origin we can safely assume that the fallen angels who are said to have taught humanity the art of agriculture, civilisation and the occult were the old planetary gods.

The archangels

The seven archangels or planetary gods rule the classical planets of the Solar system — Mercury, Venus, Mars, Jupiter and Saturn — and the two luminaries, the Sun and the Moon. The latter are sometimes called the greater lights, while the planets are known as the lesser lights. The archangelic forces are as follows:

MICHAEL rules the Sun. In ancient myths he is represented by the Solar gods such as Helios, Apollo, Ra and Lugh. In some of the early matriarchal societies the Sun was regarded as feminine, a belief that survived in the Egyptian pantheon as the Solar/Fire goddess Sekmet and in Celtic myths as the Fire goddess Bridget.

As a personification of the solar energy the Archangel Michael represents the life force. In all cultures the Sun represents the creative principle whether masculine or feminine or both.

Michael's magical image is of a young man wearing a golden cloak. His amber-coloured hair streams back from a strong face and his right hand rests upon the burnished hilt of a golden sword. The overall impression of this magical image is one of controlled spiritual power.

The Archangel Michael can be invoked in all matters associated with career, sports, personal finance, ambition, bureaucracy, officialdom and the health of the physical body. In common with Raphael he is a healing angel.

GABRIEL is the archangel of the Moon. Although the archangels are usually visualized as masculine in gender they are in fact androgynous having the potential of both sexes. As aspects of the life force they can take on either masculine or feminine characteristics. Gabriel is therefore represented in the old pagan religions by Moon goddesses such as Diana, Selene, Hathor, Hecate and Ceridwen.

There is some evidence of male Lunar deities such as Thoth and Sin. These Moon gods may have borrowed their attributes from earlier

Lunar goddesses where patriarchy replaced the prehistoric matriarchal culture.

The magical image of Gabriel is a mature man who wears the curved crescent of the waxing Moon on his forehead. This lunar symbol covers the third eye which is the source of psychic powers. Gabriel wears a silver cloak which reflects the light as does crystal glass.

Gabriel can be invoked for an increase in all things. Specifically, he has rulership over psychic powers, astral travel, conception, dreams, childbirth, all matters connected with women, travel by sea, the home and the imagination.

RAPHAEL is the planetary ruler of Mercury. He was known to the ancient Greeks as Hermes, to the Romans as Mercuri who was the messenger of the gods, to the Celts as Ogma, to the Egyptians as Thoth (pronounced Tehuti) and to the Northern Europeans as Odin or Woden.

The magical image of Raphael is a young man clothed as a pilgrim or traveller. He wears a yellow cloak, a broad rimmed hat with a feather in it, winged sandals and carries a staff entwined with two snakes, the symbol of the divine healer.

Raphael should be invoked in rituals involving healing, communication, travel, young people, education, business contracts, commercial selling, writing and self-expression. As Hermes is also the god of thieves his aid can be requested to help find stolen goods or lost property. On his highest level Raphael represents the spiritual guide or mentor who helps the person who is just beginning his/her journey on the occult path.

ANAEL is the Archangel of Venus. He/she is represented by the ancient fertility goddesses such as Aphrodite, Astarte, Isis and Frigga. His pagan male aspect is best represented by Eros whose arrows of desire captivate lovers.

Anael's magical image is a youth who seems to be neither male or female but combines the beauty of both sexes. He wears a long green cloak and his long black hair is banded by a ringlet of wild flowers and roses.

The Archangel Anael can be invoked for all matters to do with romantic love, harmony, friendship, pleasure, marital affairs, music, the arts and beauty. This angelic force represents nature as the manifestation of the divine material world. Meditation on this planetary energy can bring the magician into contact with the green goddess of nature, sometimes known as the Lady of Wild Things.

SAMUEL is the archangel of Mars. In pagan times he was associated with the gods of war such as Ares, Mars and Tiw. He represents the destructive aspect of the life force which, when channelled correctly, can be used for constructive purposes.

The magical image of Samuel is a tall man wearing a red cloak. His hair is held in place by a gold band on which is engraved a pentagram or five-pointed star. His strong hands rest on the hilt of a broadsword whose blade is decorated with runic sigils.

Samuel can be invoked for anything to do with acts of physical courage or machinery. He grants the ability of manual dexterity, craftsmanship and proctects against danger from fire and violence.

SACHIEL is the archangel of Jupiter. In ancient mythology he was the sky father known as Zeus, Jove, Dagda, Ptah and Thor. Sachiel represents the masculine phallic power which brings fertility and material abundance.

The magic image of Sachiel is a well-built older man. He wears a purple cloak decorated with gold coins as depicted in the Minor Arcana suit of the Tarot cards.

The Archangel Sachiel has rulership over all matters relating to material wealth, social eminence, political power, big business, gambling, important friendships and all legal and insurance matters. He can be invoked for assistance in all financial matters.

CASSIEL rules Saturn. In the ancient religions he is depicted as the god Chronos, Pluto and Anubis who are all deities associated with time, the underworld and death. He is also associated with the Greek goddesses known as the Fates and the Norse goddesses the Norns who are weavers of humanity's destiny. One of the Cassiel's titles is the Lord of Time and he represents the cosmic force of destiny, wyrd or fate.

Cassiel's magical image is a stern-looking man dressed in a long black cloak. Sometimes he carries a staff and an hourglass to symbolise his rulership over time.

This archangel can be invoked for all matters concerning property, old people, wills and legacies, karma, death, land, agriculture and long-standing health ailments connected with old age. In dealing with Cassiel it should be remembered that time is not linear but cyclic. Death is not the end of the human personality but the transformation to a new state of being.

When the aspiring magician invokes any of these planetary forces he should remember that they are personifications of the archetypal energies associated with each planet. These archetypal energies can be described as follows.

The planetary forces

SUN ☉ The dot within the circle is the potential of human spirit or consciousness within the universe. It is also the magician or self-aware individual following any spiritual path who is symbolically the centre of his/her own magical universe, just as the Sun is the spiritual and material centre of our Solar system.

The Sun represents both the pure essence of the life force and the higher self which is exalted in true magic. Once you take your first steps on the magical path you take on a great responsibility because your actions could have an effect on others.

It can also be a lonely path for it is the way of the individual who must stand apart from his fellows. Those around you will not understand the new path you are walking and if you are wise you will keep silent about your activities when in their company.

Increasingly, you will be thrown back on your own resources and it will take great powers of perseverance to pursue your chosen goal under such circumstances. The invocation of the Solar planetary influence can help for it provides energy, will-power and self-confidence.

MOON ☽ The symbol of the crescent Moon is a half circle which represents the subconscious mind. We have now seen how magic works through the medium of the subconscious: the realms of dreams, psychic visions, hidden desires and the imagination.

As we know the Moon has no light of its own but merely reflects the rays of the Sun. However these rays are changed by contact with the Moon and moonlight has a very different effect on the human mind from sunshine. In both astrology and magic the Moon represents the hidden side of the human personality which under normal circumstances is not revealed to the outside world.

In general most magical work is hidden (occult) and is performed out of sight in privacy. It is an old adage the magic which is practised in the public gaze will not be so successful as private workings. This belief may date back to the old days of persecution when it was impossible to work openly.

In esoteric tradition the Moon is linked with the widely held doctrine of reincarnation or the rebirth of the soul in a succession of different physical bodies. According to some arcane beliefs, when the spirit leaves the body after death it travels to the Lunar world to be reborn. In the old pagan religions we have seen that the Full Moon was one of the mystical symbols of the Great Mother Goddess who, according to the oldest creation myths, gave birth to the universe.

When the magician uses Lunar energies he is dealing with the ebb and flow of potent psychic forces. As we saw in the chapter on Moon magic the Lunar tides have both a psychic and physical affect on humans, animals and flora. It is therefore natural that occultly the Moon should symbolise the subconscious mind of the awakened person who can use it to bring hidden desires into manifestation.

MERCURY   ☿   The symbol of this fast-moving planet which is the closest to the Sun is composed of three different sigils. They are a half circle, representing the human mind, surmounted on a circle, symbolising spiritual consciousness, which in turn stands on a cross, representing the material plane.

This Mercurian symbol is a concise glyph of the mind, body and spirit. It is the fusion of these which is the ultimate goal of the higher types of magical training.

As Mercury moves quickly around the Sun it is not surprising that in classical mythology the planetary energy or god form associated with it was identified as the divine messenger. In Roman and Greek myths the gods Mercuri and Hermes were messengers of the gods.

The earliest magicians, the prehistoric shamans, were regarded by the tribal peoples who consulted them as special emissaries who had the ability to communicate with the spirit world. This communication was a two-way system for the shaman could bring back messages from the realm of the gods and pass their wisdom on to his human colleagues.

The planetary influence of Mercury teaches the aspiring magician that even though he may take his first tentative steps on the magical path for self-centred reasons, this emphasis will be short-lived. The magician soon learns that he has a wider responsibility. Service to the rest of humanity is a very important aspect of the true magical path.

Mercury is the great communicator passing on ideas, news and information. In the occult perspective the magician is the person who, like the ancient shaman, acts as a go-between, bridging the artificial barrier humanity has created between the material and spiritual worlds. This planetary energy signifies spiritual understanding and, because the Mercurial keynote is communication, the responsibility of the magician is to pass on this understanding to others.

VENUS ♀ The symbol of Venus, the evening and morning star which is esoterically the sister planet of Earth, is the circle, representing spirit, balanced on the equal-armed cross of the elements symbolising the material plane.

In ancient Egypt this Venus symbol was the ankh ♀ which represents the union of male and female. The ankh was universally adopted by the 'flower children' of the '60s who, echoing its Venusian connection, called it the love or peace cross. Today the planetary glyph of Venus is used in biology to signify the female.

Venus is regarded as the twin soul of the Earth. The concept of twin souls is a very ancient one based upon the esoteric belief that originally the human race was androgynous. At some point in the distant past early humanity divided into two sexes, so human souls continue on the cycle of birth, death and rebirth until such time as they are incarnated in the same time period as their twin souls and become reunited.

Obviously such a belief is open to abuse. This especially happens when people who fall in love project their anima (the female aspect of the male psyche) or their animus (the male apect of the female psyche) on to their lovers and think they have found their long-lost twin soul. It is the negative influence of Venus which creates this type of sexual infatuation which can be very destructive for everyone who becomes entangled in it.

On a more positive level, the Venusian planetary influence

represents the natural human desire of uniting the opposites. This can be understood in magical terms as the balancing of the male and female principles within the psyche of the magician. This union of opposites in what is called the sacred marriage and is symbolised by the sigil of the sword in the chalice.

The magician can use the planetary force of Venus in all matters which are connected with love. This can refer to romantic love between two people or the broader form of love which embraces the brotherhood of humanity.

MARS ♂ The symbol of Mars is formed by the circle of spirit surmounted by the arrow which represents the masculine aspect of the life force. This Martian glyph is used in biology to represent the male.

Mars is the red planet and that is the colour which signifies the life force. The Neolithic people buried their dead smeared in red ochre in the belief that this symbolic colour of the life force ensured that the soul of the dead person would be reborn in another body.

In the ancient times blood was regarded as sacred because of its colour and the practice of making sacrifices to appease the Divine originated in the belief that blood transmitted the life force. In our enlightened age we know that sacrificial offerings are cruel and unnecessary; the only true sacrifice is that made by the enlightened soul incarnating on the altar of material existence.

In some respects the Martian planetary influence is the opposite to the Venusian. In ancient mythology Mars was the god of war and within this martial image is hidden a great truth. If things stagnate and degenerate they must be swept away if any progress is to be made. In this sense the planetary energy of Mars represents the destroyer who cleanses and purifies so that a new beginning or cycle can commence.

Sacrifice on its highest spiritual level is the transmutation of energy into a different form. Following the occult path the aspiring magician may be called upon by the powers-that-be to make a number of sacrifices, some of which may be small but others will test the character and inner strength of the seeker.

How the individual reacts to such situations will determine how he will progress on the magical path. Whatever happens, the magician will be changed by the experience which is the transmutation of the sacrificial act. In some ways the planetary energy of Mars is a blind force, yet it cannot escape being the instrument of the powerful destiny that is the controlling influence in the universe.

The Martian force can be invoked by the magician who lacks the energy or motivation to act decisively in any given situation. The planetary force of Mars provides the magician with hidden reserves of physical, mental and spiritual energy.

JUPITER ♃ The symbol for the Jovian planetary energy is a subtle form of the half circle, the human mind, and the cross of the elements. On an esoteric level it signifies the ability of human consciousness to organise and rule the material world.

When we examined the rulership of the Archangel Sachiel, who is aligned with the planet Jupiter, we saw that he had dominion over political power and legal matters. Through ancient association with the old sky gods Sachiel is also the patron of royalty.

Politics, the law and the monarchy are all aspects of the material power-base which rules society. The Jovian planetary influence is therefore connected with the formation and maintenance of what is sometimes popularly called the Establishment.

This suggests a rigid framework which is almost dictatorial in nature yet Jupiter represents the benevolent dictator who has the best interest of his subjects paramount in his actions. The wise old king who ruled with compassion and the wisdom of experience was a powerful image in societies which worshipped the sky gods.

This belief in a wise ruler was translated into the worship of the Divine King who was the human representation of the sky god on Earth. His omnipotence was limited by the fact that he was often the consort of the Great Mother Goddess whose feminine influence modified any attempt by him to become a bloodthirsty dictator who sacrificed his subjects to his own personal whims, amibition and lust for power.

Reflecting this lack of rigidity, the keynote of Jupiter is expansion. This is represented by the material abundance which is one of the gifts Sachiel brings to those who invoke his assistance because, as well as temporal power, Jupiter rules spiritual expansion and development too.

Meditation on this aspect of the planetary force of Jupiter will enable the magician to broaden his intellectual and spiritual horizons. The invocation of the Jovian influence will create new areas of awareness and encourage the magician to be more philosophical and tolerant towards others' points of view. By using these positive energies the magician realises that a bright future awaits if he but has the courage to grasp the chances offered by Jupiter.

SATURN ♄ The astrological symbol of Saturn is the cross of matter superimposed over the half circle of the human mind. This indictes that Saturn can have a limiting or restrictive influence on the human personality and in astrology Saturn is sometimes regarded as a malefic planet.

On the esoteric level Saturn represents the role played in human affairs by the power of fate, destiny or the wyrd. The latter is an old Anglo-Saxon word for destiny from which we derive the term 'weird'.

In our description of the magical image of the Saturnian Archangel Cassiel the similarities between him and Old Father Time were noted. The grim reaper with his hour-glass and scythe is another image personifying the planetary influence of this slow-moving planet.

Saturn is traditionally the planet of old age. Its keynotes are resistance, limitation, conservatism and contraction. None of these influences should be regarded as totally negative, however.

Even the most active magician must take some time off from his workings to take stock of the situation or just for reflective purposes. Life cannot be led at high speed for long periods of time. The person who tries to do so will only succeed in burning out his life energies, whether he is an ordinary person living a mundane life or a magician following the occult path.

There will be periods during the magical apprenticeship when the requirement for action on the inner levels will diminish. A point must be reached where the magician must access his progress in relation to what is being achieved on the magical and/or psychic levels. Saturn teaches this lesson.

The Saturnine planetary influence is also karmic in nature. This aspect can be very important in some forms of practical magic, especially when the magician is working for material gain on the physical plane. Although magic has the ability to attract material things to the practitioner's sphere there are very few rich magicians around.

The reason for this can be found in the laws of karma which influence the experiences of the soul in each incarnation. As a person who is spiritually aware, the magician is not obsessed with the acquisition of material objects and rightly regards them as useful tools to make life easier.

The planetary influence of the Saturn force also manifests in the morality of magic. It should be emphasised very strongly that it is totally wrong to use magical energies to do harm to any living creature or to interfere in the free-will of others.

The esoteric traditions are explicit about what happens to anyone who ignores this fact. It is a widespread magical belief that the magical energy raised to perform such acts will return threefold to the sender. This returning energy will create serious disruptions in the magician's life and incur karmic debts which will have to be paid for either in this life or the next.

The energies raised in magical workings are neutral and are neither good or evil. It is the application to which they are put by the individual that determines their potential, positively or negatively.

Saturn is the testing planet and magicians who invoke its planetary influence must learn to live with the results. As Saturn is associated with karma and responsibility the magician must at all times be willing to take the consequences of any magical action. If you consider this fact very carefully before invoking the Saturnian energies all will be well. A lack of detail (another Saturnian trait) will soon bring you back to reality with a bump.

These then are the seven major planetary forces or archetypes which the magician can utilise. The method of invoking such forces will depend on the natural inclination of the magician. A list of magical correspondences relating to each planetary force is given at the end of this book. Careful study of these correspondences will assist you to set up a ritual correctly.

A ritual for love

As an example, say the magician wished to perform a ritual for love. This involves the invocation of the planetary energy of Venus. By consulting the list of magical correspondences you can establish exactly what is required for the correct performance of such a ritual.

Preferably the ritual should be performed either when Venus is well aspected astrologically or when the waxing Moon is in one of the zodiacal signs ruled by Venus. If the ritual is urgent you may not wish to wait until the astrological aspects are right and in such cases should perform the ritual when the Moon is waxing on a Friday, the day sacred to Venus. Information on Lunar phases and planetary aspects is published each month in PREDICTION. You do not need to be an expert astrologer to practise magic but some basic knowledge of the subject is essential if you are going to take advantage of positive aspects and avoid days when the planets are poorly aspected.

The planetary colours of Venus are blue or green, so the candles you burn should be of that hue and your altar may also be covered in a similarly coloured cloth. A single red rose in a copper container can be placed on the altar. If you are financially secure enough to own different robes for the planetary colours then wear a green or blue one to match the candles and altar cloth.

You can either invoke the Archangel Anael or one of the pagan goddesses such as Aphrodite or Frigga to represent the planetary energy. Which god form you choose will depend on your own religious outlook.

Read as many books on the old pagan gods as you can, especially illustrated children's books of myths. Build a mental image of each of the gods and goddesses from the Greek, Roman, Celtic, Norse, Egyptian or even Hindu pantheons and write verbal descriptions of these in a notebook for future reference.

Use these word pictures to visualize the god form mentally for, by doing so, you are symbolically contacting the planetary influence it respresents. Such images may be mythical yet you will find that they exist within our multi-dimensional universe as very real personifications of the life force.

How your approach the actual invocation of the planetary energy is a matter of choice. Please ignore those medieval grimoires which depict the magus commanding archangels to appear within his magical triangle of art. Such fanciful practices have only existed within the imaginations of would-be magicians and the dusty volumes they wrote about their fantasies.

The safest approach to the contact of the planetary forces is to visualize a mental image of the god, goddess or angel which represents the power you wish to invoke. A spoken petition can then be recited stating the purpose of the invocation. This does not need to be in flowery language but should be as simple and direct as possible.

Some magicians prefer to use a physical representation of the god form in their rituals, believing that these sacred images become empowered with the energy of the invoked deity. This is a legitimate form of working but impractical unless you concentrate on one particular pantheon of deities in your magical workings.

It does not matter if you call upon the archangels or the classical gods of European mythology because, as the well-known occultist Dion Fortune once said, 'All the Gods are one God'. One important point to remember is not to mix god forms from different religions in the same ritual.

Through its use of astrology and the invocation of the pagan gods and goddesses, the use of magical correspondences and its emphasis on both the material and spiritual, planetary magic provides an overall view of the magical philosophy expressed throughout the pages of this book. We have examined various types of magic in these pages but which one you decide to practise will depend entirely on what you feel most comfortable with and the purpose of the ritual you are going to perform.

This book has been written for the individual working as a solo magician. It should be obvious that a working partner or additional people can be introduced into the process to give it added energy. Some people who step on the magical path seek the company of others and this will usually involve entry into a group of practising magicians.

Such a step obviously has its advantages because the experienced can act as guides to those with less knowledge of practical magical techniques. There can be dangers in invoking archetypal images and safety in numbers applies to magic just as any other risky venture in life.

However, commonsense and the right moral attitude to your magical workings will ensure that no harm will come to you. It should be emphasised here that none of the magical techniques or pathworkings in this book are unsafe to use, all can be performed without question or trepidation.

There is nothing to be afraid of in this book. The sinister image accredited to magic is a falsehood built up by centuries of prejudice and anti-occult propaganda by the vested interests of those who had their own selfish reasons for the destruction of esoteric knowledge.

With the dawning of the Aquarian Age, preceded by the Grand Conjunction of planets in Aquarius in February 1962, attitudes to the hidden side of life have changed dramatically. As the Aquarian influence grows in strength with each passing decade the magical outlook will become more and more influential.

As a practising magician it is your destiny to be a pioneer in the New Age of spiritual illumination which at present is only in its infancy.

Table of Magical Correspondences

Planetary Magic

The Sun

Planetary influence: rules success, ambition, career matters, healing, personal finance, bureaucracy and officialdom, sport.
Day of the week: Sunday
Archangel: Michael
God forms: Apollo, Lugh, Ra, Helios, Sekhmet
Zodiacal sign: Leo (July 21–August 21)
Element: Fire
Planetary colour: Gold
Planetary metal: Gold
Incense: Frankincense
Flower: Marigold, sunflower, heliotrope
Animal: Lion
Bird: Hawk

The Moon

Planetary influence: Rules psychic powers, dreams, childbirth, women, travel by sea, the home, imagination, reincarnation.
Day of the week: Monday
Archangel: Gabriel
God forms: Diana, Artemis, Selene, Hathor, Hecate, Ceridwen

Zodiacal sign: Cancer (June 21–July 20)
Element: Water
Planetary colour: Silver
Planetary metal: Silver
Incense: Jasmine
Flower: Night-scented stock, convolvulus
Animal: Dog, crab
Bird: Owl

Mercury

Planetary influence: Rules communications, intelligence, memory, education, healing, travel, business contracts, writing, acting and finding lost or stolen property.
Day of the week: Wednesday
Archangel: Raphael
God forms: Mercury, Hermes, Thoth, Ogma, Odin, Athene
Zodiacal signs: Gemini (May 21–June 20) and Virgo (August 22–September 22)
Element: Air
Planetary colour: Yellow
Planetary metal: Quicksilver
Incense: Sandalwood
Flower: Fern, broom, aniseed
Animal: Monkey
Bird: Magpie

Venus

Planetary influence: Rules romantic love, beauty, pleasure, harmony, marital affairs, twin souls, friendship, music and the arts.
Day of the week: Friday
Archangel: Anael
God forms: Aphrodite, Astarte, Isis, Frigga, Eros
Zodiacal signs: Libra (September 23–October 22) and Taurus (April 21–May 20)
Element: Air
Planetary colour: Green or blue
Planetary metal: Copper

Incense: Rosewood
Flower: Rose
Animal: Cat
Bird: Dove

Mars

Planetary influence: Rules machinery, courage, manual dexterity and offers protection against danger from fire and volcano.
Day of the week: Tuesday
Archangel: Samuel
God forms: Mars, Ares, Tiw
Zodiacal signs: Aries (March 21–April 20) and Scorpio (October 23–November 22)
Element: Fire
Planetary colour: Red
Planetary metal: Iron
Incense: Pine
Flowers: Thistles and nettles
Animal: Ram
Bird: Falcon

Jupiter

Planetary influence: Rules material wealth, social eminence, political power, big business, gambling, games of chance, important friendships, legal and insurance matters.
Day of the week: Thursday
Archangel: Sachiel
God forms: Jupiter, Zeus, Thor, Dagda, Ptah
Zodiacal signs: Sagittarius (November 23–December 20) and Pisces (February 19–March 20)
Element: Fire
Planetary colour: Purple
Planetary metal: Tin
Incense: Cedar
Flower: Lilac
Animal: Elephant
Bird: Eagle

Saturn

Planetary influence: Rules property, old people, karma, death, legacies, long-standing health ailments and agriculture.

Day of the week: Saturday

Archangel: Cassiel

God forms: Chronos, Pluto, Seb, Anubis, the Norns

Zodiacal signs: Capricorn (December 21–January 19) and Aquarius (January 20–February 18)

Element: Earth

Planetary colour: Black

Planetary metal: Lead

Incense: Myrhh

Flower: Chrysanthemum

Animal: Tortoise

Bird: Parrot

Elemental Magic

Water

Elemental influence: Emotions, intuition, the inner self

Elemental guardian: Niksa

Elemental spirits: Undines

Direction: West

Time of day: Dusk

Season: Autumn

Colours: Silver or blue

Zodiacal signs: Cancer, Scorpio, and Pisces

Magical tools: Chalice

Meditation symbol: Flowing river or waterfall

Earth

Elemental influence: Growth, nature, material abundance, fertility

Elemental guardian: Ghob

Elemental spirits: Gnomes

Direction: North

Time of day: Midnight
Season: Winter
Colours: Black or brown
Zodiacal signs: Taurus, Virgo and Capricorn
Magical tool: Pentacle
Meditation symbol: Standing stone

Air

Elemental influence: Concentration, intellect, communication, knowledge
Elemental guardian: Paralda
Elemental spirits: Sylphs
Direction: East
Time of day: Dawn
Season: Spring
Colour: Yellow
Zodiacal signs: Gemini, Libra and Aquarius
Magical tool: Wand
Meditation symbol: Mountain peak

Fire

Elemental influence: Energy, courage, will-power, purification
Elemental guardian: Djinn
Direction: South
Time of day: Noon
Season: Summer
Colour: Gold or orange
Zodiacal signs: Aries, Leo and Sagittarius
Magical tool: Sword
Meditation symbol: A fire blazing on a stone altar

The combination of the four elemental forces is the fifth element of Spirit
which is represented in magical correspondences as follows.

Spirit

Elemental influence: Transformation, immanence
Elemental guardian: —

Elemental spirits: —
Time of day: Beyond time & space
Season: the Wheel of the Year
Colour: Brilliant white
Zodiacal signs: The twelve signs of the zodiac
Magical tool: The altar
Meditation symbol: An equal-armed cross in a circle

Index

prediction

THE MAGAZINE FOR ASTROLOGY AND THE OCCULT

... is a popular style magazine for those interested in astrology and all aspects of the occult. It is published on the second Friday of each month and contains regular features on the Tarot, graphology, palmistry, dream interpretations, book reviews and a 16-page astrology section including Sun sign forecasts for the month ahead as well as feature articles on a wide range of occult and related subjects.

68 pages or more monthly, illustrated and carrying advertisements—including a directory of psychics and consultants, groups, societies etc—PREDICTION represents incredible value for money and offers readers several services including two free ones: Occult Question Time and Personal Classifieds, so why not buy a copy now?

Available from all leading newsagents. In case of difficulty, write to Prediction Magazine, Link House, Dingwall Ave, Croydon CR9 2TA. Telephone 01·686 2599 ⧓ A Link House Publication